E 500

MODERN TRENDS IN DOCUMENTATION

Modern Trends in Documentation

*Proceedings of a Symposium held at the
University of Southern California
April 1958*

Edited by
DR. MARTHA BOAZ

DEAN, SCHOOL OF LIBRARY SCIENCE,
UNIVERSITY OF SOUTHERN CALIFORNIA

PERGAMON PRESS LTD.

NEW YORK · LONDON · PARIS · LOS ANGELES

1959

HARVARD - YENCHING LIBRARY
2 Divinity Avenue
Cambridge 38, Massachusetts

Coop

OCT 20 1960

9770/09

PERGAMON PRESS INC.
122 *East 55th Street, New York 22, N.Y.*
P.O. Box 47715, Los Angeles, California.

PERGAMON PRESS LTD.
4 & 5 *Fitzroy Square, London W*.1.

PERGAMON PRESS S.A.R.L.
24, *Rue des Écoles, Paris V*ᵉ.

Z 699 .L6

Los Angeles (Calif.).
 University of Southern

Modern trends in
 documentation

Copyright
©
Pergamon Press Inc.
1959

Library of Congress Card Number 59–10081.

Set in Monotype Baskerville by Santype Ltd., Salisbury,
and printed by Wyman & Sons Ltd., Fakenham, in Great Britain

Contents

Contents

vi

Foreword

MARTHA BOAZ

Dean, School of Library Science
University of Southern California

THIS symposium on Documentation, sponsored by the School of Library Science of the University of Southern California, April 9–11, 1958, was held for the purpose of stimulating interest in information retrieval.

Due to the increase in knowledge and the vast quantity of published material, the matter of keeping informed even in a specialized field has become an enormous problem. The necessity for "keeping up" with recorded information has posed a problem for specialists, research workers, and librarians. The answer is being sought in an information retrieval system or systems. Questions involving documentation and information retrieval are constantly being asked, research is in progress, but definitive conclusions have not been found. No one can predict the library world of the future, but indications point to a new technology, different from that now in use. Mechanized systems for searching, correlating and synthesizing recorded knowledge will, without doubt, be in general usage in the not too distant future. There is urgent need for effective, efficient and practical methods for retrieving information, which may be achieved with a minimum expenditure of time, money and energy.

The papers presented at this symposium represent the thinking of various persons in different types of institutions or job situations— all interested in information retrieval in one form or another.

As the separate section headings of the printed program indicated, the following general topics were planned for the three day symposium:

    I. The Problem of Information Retrieval. Past Methods and Failures. Semantics. The Individual Needs of Each Library served by An Information Retrieval System.
    II. Problems in Locating Information.
    III. Mechanical Translation
        Linguistic Analysis and Language Data Processing.
        Automatic Computers in Machine Translation.
    IV. Automatic Encoding.
    V. Application of High-Speed Computers to Information Retrieval.
    VI. Data retrieval with microfilm, magnacard, and minicard.

Following the formal sessions, the last afternoon was devoted to a panel discussion centered around the topic: "Planning for the Future".

There is great variety in the presentation and style of the different papers. This usually follows in a symposium due to the very nature of the subject matter and to the variety of human nature. The informal discussions following each meeting are not included in these proceedings.

Persons attending the symposium commented on the variety of knowledge, the diversity of background, and the intensity of interest of the audience and of the speakers. It is hoped that this meeting will result in greater interest and accelerated progress in the field of documentation and information retrieval.

Especial thanks should be given to Mrs. Sophia White, Librarian of the Electrodata Division, Burroughs Corporation, who gave invaluable advice and help in planning the entire program. Other members of the planning committee to whom thanks are due are Margaret Anderson, RAND Corporation; Doris Banks, Ground Systems Division, Hughes Aircraft; Albert P. Bradley, Atomics International Division, North American Aviation, Inc.; Benjamin de Gorter, Riker Laboratories, Inc., and Rexal Drug Company; Dana H. Johnson, Technical Library, Hughes Aircraft; Edythe Moore, American Potash and Chemical Corporation; Nell Steinmetz, Pacific Aeronautical Library.

Specialized Planning for Information Retrieval

ROBERT S. MEYER

formerly of Herner, Meyer & Company
Washington, D.C.

AT THIS Symposium, we will be privileged to hear from many of the leading figures in the information retrieval field. They will describe for us the latest systems, equipment, and research activities designed to store and retrieve information faster, more efficiently, and in greater quantities then ever before. But before we look into the exciting world of magnetic tape, memory drums, and electronic brains which modern technology has developed for us, we might pause for a moment to consider the often-forgotten man of information retrieval, the user.

The reason we should devote some thought to the user of our information system is an obvious one: the information system, and indeed the entire information program of an organization, should exist, in the final analysis, just to serve the needs of its users. Librarians are members of a profession dedicated to the service of their patrons and sponsors. Thus, libraries are a means to an end, not an end in themselves. The end being sought is, of course, communication from one person to another, the library program playing an important role of middle-man in this process. The degree of success we achieve in our field can be measured only in terms of the degree of satisfaction felt by those we are employed to serve.

1

Of all the various activities in which the modern librarian engages, that of information storage and retrieval is thought by many to be the most important and the most characteristic of this profession. The practice of information retrieval, then, must be dedicated to the same general objectives as its parent profession. And a system of storing and retrieving information, whatever its degree of simplicity or complexity, should be similarly thought of as a means to an end, not as an end in itself. In this case, the end being sought is the finding of pieces of information on request, once they have been acquired and stored in a collection. The degree of success achieved by the information system is measured by its effectiveness in finding answers to questions put to it, coupled with its efficiency in supplying this service at a reasonable speed and at a reasonable price.

Thus, the library, the information program, and the storage and retrieval system cannot be evaluated in a vacuum, but must always take into account the users of the particular services in question. It has been said that a tree crashing in the forest makes no sound if there is no ear present to hear it, and that a work of art has no beauty unless there is a mind present to appreciate it. In the same way, an information system which is not being used effectively and efficiently to serve the needs of its user-group, regardless of the capabilities or potentialities the system may possess, makes no real sound and has no real beauty in our business of communication.

If we are seeking an explanation for the frequent failures of our information systems to satisfy their users, we shall find it largely in our failure to acquire and utilize an understanding of the needs, desires, and habits of the particular group to be served. An example to illustrate this point is found in the difficulties experienced by many special librarians who have tried to use a general classification scheme, such as the Dewey Decimal or Library of Congress schedules, for the shelving and subject control of their collections. Since these broad classifications try to cover all the world's knowledge for all the world's users, they present the special librarian with too many choices of categories on too broad a level for the specific collection and users involved. The solution often reached in such cases is that the special librarian expands a small portion of the general classification scheme to handle the collection. Thus, without formally setting out to do so, such librarians are actually designing their own classification systems to compensate for the inability of the general schemes to take into account the needs of their special libraries.

In the majority of cases, the problem is not that our existing technology is insufficiently advanced to provide the mechanisms we need for effective information handling. In fact, librarianship, as well as most other phases of our life, suffers more from our inability to assimilate and keep pace with advancing technological developments than from any shortcomings in the technology itself. The technology available today is already adequate to achieve great improvements in the information services we render our constituents. And, as we shall learn from the other speakers on the program, information technology, like most other technologies, continues to race even further ahead. In short, the practical problem we face in this area is the proper selection and application of the systems and equipment now available to us, and to do this properly we must understand clearly the elements of our own individual working environment.

Now one might ask whether different library situations are really very individualistic, or pretty much the same from place to place. The answer, at least for special libraries, lies in the very word "special". In these installations the collection is special, the users are special, and the uses to which the information is put are special. Although we can recognize a number of general traits of special library users as a group, there are very few generalizations we can make about the nature and content of their information retrieval apparatus. Each installation should properly have individual analysis and planning to suit its unique circumstances.

The emphasis placed on the importance and necessity of treating each special library as a unique entity should not lead one to the inference that there is no basic body of knowledge useful to the special librarian. On the contrary, a sound understanding of library principles and practices will enable the special librarian to serve his clientele even more effectively. Moreover, we should not

3

think of this necessity to examine each library situation individually as a failure for the field of librarianship. It is just the opposite. To be able to examine an individual situation in the light of our general principles and experience, to prescribe an individual course of action, and to realize thereby a higher degree of satisfaction to our clientele, is the most truly professional phase of any activity. It is the counterpart of the medical profession's diagnosis and treatment, drawing upon a great body of accumulated knowledge to assist a specific patient with a specific ailment.

Now just who are these people to be served? Simple though it may sound, this question often takes some work and some thought for the individual librarian to solve. Conferences with supervisors and top management are necessary to define with some accuracy the responsibility of the library or information program to various groups inside and outside the organization. In addition to serving the technical or professional people in the institution, the role of the library in serving such groups as management personnel, non-technical departments, company branch offices, outside organizations, and the general public must be determined as a matter of policy. We should also include as users the members of the information staff themselves, who, while acting on behalf of their clientele, are often the heaviest users of the library.

There are three common pitfalls to be avoided in thinking about the composition of our user-audience. The first pitfall is to assume that the people now using our facilities are representative of the entire user-group we are expected to serve. This might omit from our consideration many persons who, for one reason or another, are not now active library users but who are within the library's responsibility. Some of these non-users may just not be aware of library services which could be of assistance to them. Others may have tried at some earlier time to make use of the library's facilities without success, with the result that they feel no desire to try again. It is perhaps unnecessary to point out that these groups of non-active library users, who often far outnumber the active ones, may be just as important to us in planning our library program as are the active users. It could even be argued that the non-active ones should be of greater concern to us, since the library and information facilities are not presently of any assistance to them, while the active users are presumably deriving some degree of benefit from our services.

A second trap we must guard against falling into is to assume that the ways in which our clientele presently use our information services are the ways they prefer. We have to keep in mind that we ourselves, in furnishing the information facilities to our users, will inevitably condition to some extent the use that is made of those facilities. Unless we ask our users about everything in our set-up from one end to the other, keeping our own assumptions out of the picture, we may overlook some possible areas of improvement. As an example of this point, a portion of a particular special library in Washington consisted of foreign-language books which were shelved alphabetically by author while those in English were arranged by subject. The librarian maintained that this situation was satisfactory, since the users very rarely did any subject browsing in the foreign-language portion of the collection. The point we can observe here, of course, is that the users could not possibly browse the foreign-language shelves by subject, since those items were in random subject order. Upon questioning the users, it was quickly made plain that one of their major desires was for those foreign-language books to be arranged in subject order on the shelves.

The third error to be avoided in thinking about our clientele is to regard the library user as some sort of inferior being. He is sometimes thought of as possessing the qualities of childlike ignorance, gross stupidity, and complete lack of understanding of library practices and problems. Moreover, he is often troublesome, meddlesome, irritable, and unreasonable. Above all, he doesn't even know what kinds of information he needs, how he acquires it, or how he uses it, so trying to make him a part of library planning is a fruitless waste of time. In short, he is practically a total loss to society, and the library would be far better off if it could be allowed to operate without any users coming in at all. The sad part of all this is that too often this result is just what is achieved by such attitudes.

As has already been mentioned, however, it is these very people for whom our information services are established and to whose presence we owe our existence as information specialists. And the intellectual superiority we sometimes feel toward our users is, of course, completely unjustified when we stop to think about the achievements of our times. After all, it is our users who actually are bringing about these accomplishments. And last, but by no means least, let us not sell the user short on the matter of having a clear understanding of how and why he goes about acquiring and using various kinds of information in the performance of his job. In most instances, if our methods are soundly constructed and applied, the amount of helpful and constructive information we can get from our users is truly surprising.

This brings up the subject of technique. Assuming that we have decided to plan our library program or information system to fit the requirements peculiar to our own individual environment, and assuming further that we have obtained a clear idea of the composition of the clientele we are expected to serve, what do we do next? What we are faced with, essentially, is a job of market research, which, in the commercial world, is a widely applied technique used to ensure a better customer acceptance of a product. The product we want to sell is information service, and the consumers we want to reach are our present and potential users. Just as in selling any other product, we must find out what ingredients the intended consumer would prefer included and which he would rather omit. We must also learn how he wants it packaged and delivered. To help us reach a clearer understanding, we should also become familiar with his reasons or motivations for desiring the product, the uses to which he will put it, and other sources or methods from which he obtains or can obtain our product.

There are a number of methods we might use to elicit information which will tell us what we need to know about our audience. The choice of methods will depend largely on the size and character of the population being studied, and whether the group is physically located in a single area or is dispersed or ill-defined. Often, a combination of methods is very productive and at the same time provides a kind of check on the validity of the findings. Some methods which have been used in designing information systems to determine the requirements, viewpoints, and language of the user are: (1) detailed interviews with a cross-section of the user population, (2) observations of day-to-day activities and problems of users over a period of time, (3) the analysis of representative samples of the writings of users, and (4) the analysis of a cross-section of reference questions actually arising from the users.

The interview method has the feature of bringing you face-to-face with your library user. The depth of detail and understanding which can be derived from this method cannot be matched by any other. To achieve good results, however, the questionnaires must be well constructed and carefully thought out. The questions must all be thoroughly field-tested so as to be clear, meaningful, and unbiased. They should concern themselves more with facts than with opinions, should be as specific as possible, and should make as few assumptions as possible. Answers to questions concerning what the respondent has actually done in the recent past are more reliable than those covering what he thinks he might do in the future. Interviewing technique must be practised until it becomes direct and impartial while still cordial and friendly.

It is entirely probable that the benefits to be gained from the interview study will exceed the immediate objectives of learning about your users. For one thing, the user often is asked to think about things he was never particularly conscious of before, and finds as a result that his awareness of his own activities is increased to the point where he can recognize and correct shortcomings in his own procedures. In addition, one of the greatest side-benefits of an interview market analysis is improved public relations. The survey indicates to your users that you are trying to improve their services for their own benefit, and in coming to them as a source of information to be used in this improvement program you indicate to them that you value and respect what they have to say. A third side-benefit of this procedure is the opportunity it provides for the librarian to meet this clientele on a personal basis, making for much greater mutual understanding. A fourth advantage is the opportunity for the librarian to employ a little salesmanship for the organization's information program, and thus to publicize in an effective way the present and projected services offered to the user.

Whatever methods we use, it is always advisable to enlist the support of management prior to launching the inquiry. The

7

publicity and authority which can be gained by having top management behind your study will be helpful in many ways.

There is an important precaution we must take when using any method of audience inquiry. We must make sure that the items we examine in our study, whether they be people, reference questions, publications, or anything else, are proportionately representative of the entire clientele lying within our responsibility. We must study some representatives of every department and every level of activity. For example, if some of our professional men have research assistants who do a significant amount of work in the library for their supervisors, we will want to make sure that both of these levels of use are studied.

Thus far, we have concentrated on the user as the major element of uniqueness in any individual working environment. Now it is time to turn to the information collection as the other unique factor in our planning. It goes almost without saying that a good librarian knows his collection intimately. He knows its nature and magnitude, how it got there, why it is there, where it is coming from, what is in it, who uses it and how they use it, and its strengths and short-comings. Although much of this information can best be supplied by the user, some of it will have to come from the librarian's own detailed examination of the collection. Not every single piece of literature need be examined for purposes of setting up an information system, however. A representative or random cross-section of the items in the collection will suffice, if the sample is sufficiently large.

Along with an intimate knowledge of our clientele and our collection, we must also become familiar with the various systems and devices available to us for use as aids in information retrieval. This will include the older, more traditional methods as well as the newer, more mechanized ones. In considering economic factors, we must be sure to check for input costs as well as output costs, and to watch for hidden costs, such as the need for highly trained specialist personnel or the necessity to revamp completely the existing information system we are using.

After taking all of these factors into consideration, we will be able to evaluate each information system in the light of our own particular needs more wisely and realistically than would otherwise have been possible. For example, if the librarian finds that most of his users prefer to go directly to the shelves to find useful items or to browse, he should hesitate to install a system which would require his collection to be shelved by chronological accession rather than by subject, or a system which would require everyone to use the catalog or index before getting the items desired.

Regardless of the system or method which is eventually selected, and regardless of the degree of sophistication or complexity it may possess, the purely intellectual task of designing the framework of classes, subject headings, descriptors, uniterms, or what-have-you still remains. These will be the terms which will describe the subject content of the items in the collection so that these items may be retrieved at some later time when these terms are thought to be pertinent to a user's inquiry. This operation is the most important factor in the success of the information system, and it can be accomplished only by human beings, not by machines. It is not an automatic mechanism, since human judgment is indispensable in determining the subject content of a ducument which might be useful to a particular group of people in a particular way. And it is in the construction and application of the subject analysis framework that the librarian's knowledge of his users and his collection is of crucial importance.

It is at this point that the librarians can make excellent use of another technique of market research—the consumer panel. At every stage in its construction, the subject framework is submitted to a small but representative group of the user-population for analysis and criticism. This procedure is of great importance in ensuring that the choice and arrangement of the terms in the framework reflect the language and viewpoint of the users. Another advantage lies in the ready accessibility of expert assistance in the resolving of technical language problems or questions. And not only should the system be tried out, at various stages of its development, on a group of its actual future users, but thorough tests should also be made on the items actually in the collection to be organized. When this vital job is completed in this way, the librarian can have confidence in the eventual workability of the system because it has been designed with his actual clientele and collection in mind, rather than in an intellectual ivory tower as is sometimes the case.

The librarian's role in this interplay with his user panel, by the way, should not be one of meek or passive acceptance of everything they say to him. After all, information is really the librarian's speciality, not theirs, and he must evaluate and shape what he is told in the light of his specialized knowledge. If he thinks his users are requesting something that will result in ambiguity, redundancy, or inordinate expense in the information system, he must by all means express his thoughts to them in terms that will be understandable to them. The situation is analogous to that of an architect designing a building or a home. He, like the librarian, wants to include in his structure everything the client desires within reason, but in his professional capacity he must inform the customer of structural weaknesses or unusual expenses inherent in those desires. Compromises will then be designed to approach the ideal as nearly as practicable from both points of view.

One type of subject framework which has been found to be quite satisfactory for special libraries is the tailor-made or specially-designed classification. Such schemes, when they are constructed according to the principles mentioned above and which have been discussed in greater detail in an article in *Science**, have seven basic features: (1) the subject classes and terms reflect the viewpoints and language of the users, (2) the system reflects the actual literature collection and the purposes for which it is used, (3) the classes and terms are mutually exclusive in content and meaning so as to reduce ambiguity and redundancy, (4) the number of items within classes is approximately equal and of convenient size, (5) the system is expandable to allow for new documents and new subjects, (6) the notation identifying classes is simple and constant, and (7) the grouping together of related classes reflects the habits and viewpoints of the users rather than any "natural" law. An advantage of this system is that it can be used for either manual or mechanical applications. The payoff for designing such a system is realized in greater speed

* S. HERNER and R. S. MEYER, Classifying and Indexing for the Special Library, *Science*, 125, 799–803 (1957).

of input and output, simpler operation, more consistent and effective results, and lower costs.

But this is only one system, and there are many. Some are old, some are new. Some are manual, some mechanized, some in-between. As members of the library profession, we must be familiar with them all, just as we must be acquainted with the various kinds of shelving, or copying devices, or any other piece of library equipment. The difference here, of course, is one of magnitude. Few, if any, of our library purchases will be as expensive, as difficult to change, or as important to the success of our library as the information retrieval system we install. Therefore, we must educate ourselves not only regarding the capabilities and limitations of various information retrieval systems but also on methods for studying our clienteles. We should also make use of the assistance which is available from the manufacturers and suppliers of systems, from our colleagues, and from consultants.

Meetings such as this Symposium furnish an excellent forum for the exchange of information on such topics, and a vote of thanks is due the University of Southern California School of Library Science and Dean Boaz for organizing it for us. Perhaps another way in which our educational institutions could further assist members of the library field in acquiring more knowledge about such subjects is through the initiation of more courses along these lines into the library school curriculum. The modern librarian, in order to succeed, will have to become more and more expert in these areas.

As in any expanding area of knowledge, these facets of modern librarianship require continuing research to explore the horizons opened up by each new development or finding. We need more information concerning users' needs and ways of ascertaining and meeting them. In addition, more studies are needed which make comparative evaluations of various systems for diverse applications. Another fruitful line of inquiry might lie in the study and analysis of specific installations of information systems which have failed to serve their intended purposes, seeking the underlying reasons for these failures. Research studies along the above lines can be among the most exciting and productive projects the information specialist might pursue.

To summarize in current terminology, let me say that before we blast off into outer space with a new information retrieval system for our library, let's make sure to include a study of our users somewhere in our countdown procedure. In this way our missile will have a much greater likelihood of hitting our intended target.

The Nature of
Information Retrieval

H. R. J. GROSCH

Assistant to the Director of Marketing Programs
International Business Machines Corporation

FIRST of all, we have to get a few terms straight. During the next three days, we are going to hear from people who are hardware oriented, people who are problem oriented, people who have no particular orientation but are excited about the possibilities of the interaction. I'm sure that those who are going to contribute— and all of you who are listening—don't understand the same things by the same labels. I shall make a few comments about the nature of the problem and define some terms as I use them, in the hope that as others give you meatier talks, they will at least correct my definition to theirs if they plan to use it in some other sense.

The ultimate thing we are looking for is answers to questions. We are not looking for means of building up collections of reports, books, photostats, reels of microfilm. We are looking for answers. It happens, however, that at our present stage of intellectual development—and I don't think this is a question of hardware development at all—we do not know how to ask electronic devices questions in such a form that we receive the answers we want. Now if we're asking a telephone directory for an address or a telephone number, fine; there we ask a simple question, and with a little imagination one can conceive of an automatic answering device which would give a straightforward answer. But when one wants to know about

13

the boiling point of a specified organic compound, one normally does not get the actual answer from an information retrieval system. What arrives is a notation pointing to a source document, a report, a frame of microfilm, an audible recording perhaps, which contains among other things the answer to the question you want. So I like to use the term "information retrieval" to mean exactly that— the retrieval of desired information, and I refer to the more common problem of getting back the report, the book, the microfilm frame you want, as "document retrieval".

I would like to make an aside that the original attempts in this field have not been part of the information handling or computing or data handling business at all. For instance, the initial venture that led to the Rapid Selector, by Ralph Shaw at the Department of Agriculture library, was an outstanding contribution to the graphic arts. That machine was given the number of a certain document and produced a copy of that document very rapidly and without human intervention. I consider this a novel replacement of the communication and graphic arts processes that we use in currently reproducing visual records. If the machine had sorted through a list of abstracts, indexing terms, or co-ordinates, and come out with the proper document—and, of course, this was conceptually the plan—then we would have had a true document retrieval scheme.

Now we always have to decide what our aims are. Those of you who work with collections of high value per item are in a much better position to use certain techniques than those in charge of broad collections, most items having rather dubious value, or from which you have already extracted the treasure items for hoarding separately; where the value of the collection consists in its catholicity, its breadth, its depth in time. A set of *comptes rendus* going back to seventeen hundred and something is a very valued item in a large university library, but completely worthless—at least, the older numbers are completely worthless—in a modern electronics laboratory. On the other hand, in the report collections with which many of you are concerned, each document represents many thousands of dollars worth of investigation, of experimentation, and the turnover of employees—or should I say the *promotion* of employees to positions of greater responsibility?—is such that no individual has a full knowledge of what is in these files, albeit they are not large. It is highly doubtful that our hardware potential at the present time is sufficient to evolve a single system, sub-sets of which will be capable of handling these two extremes.

Now, if in addition you go broadly into the information retrieval problem, where you want to get answers to questions and not bother with the intermediate documentation, with these questions phrased in a technology and even in a language—and I mean language in the sense of English, French, Russian—which is different from that in which the information is stored, you begin to see the really complex problems. Such problems will be tackled, and will be solved, by the technology of computing in the distant future, but they are clearly extremely expensive and extremely difficult of solution in the immediate future.

We ought also to talk about the difficulties of input. Some of you work with collections which are building up at a very rapid percentage. A library which is only five years old, even though acquiring material at a normal rate, is certainly increasing percentagewise much more rapidly than one which is essentially old. With information coming in at a very high percentage level, the problems of input to the system are not too difficult. You can afford, if necessary, to go through your back files and re-abstract, re-code, punch on to a paper tape, dictate into a standard format, whatever the magic input to the system is, all your back material. But such techniques are out of the question for a large old collection where no individual item warrants such attention. The data handling people are very much concerned with the invention of gadgets such as character sensors and page readers which will electronically scan a page of print in any type face and record the information there on more machineable media such as magnetic tape, but I doubt very much if in the next decade or two they will be capable of doing this at a price sufficiently attractive to enable an old library, one with a hundred years of holdings, to re-record all its documents. I might instance the problems that are involved even in micro-filming old documents where in most cases one does this only because the documents are in danger of falling apart. The job is done to preserve them rather than to record them in more easily accessible media.

Output in the same way is a function of the particular nature of the collection with which you are dealing. It is quite certain that the kind of output which is practical in an organization like ASTIA, the Library of Congress, the Patent Office, a very large research library such as the John Crerar for instance, is completely impractical in total cost for a small outfit, even though the cost per unit of output (page of photostat, inch of magnetic tape, or whatever) is attractive. The small shops don't have enough volume to divide into the extremely high costs of superlative printing and other output devices to get the low unit cost. As an example, one of the competitors of IBM has demonstrated a page printer capable of producing fantastic quantities of really high caliber printed material from reels of magnetic tape. One can already expect five thousand lines of printing a minute, and it is clear that one can count on an improvement factor of tenfold at least, before they run into mechanical or electronic problems. It is also clear that extensions of the photographic process will permit output devices printing hundreds of thousands of lines of information per minute. And when you get to this point, literally and seriously, the cost of the paper on which you are printing becomes the dominant item. It may therefore be very important that output devices print on something cheesy like newsprint because a high grade, high strength, uniform paper would double the cost of output. The tremendous speed of such a machine would make the cost of printing itself almost negligible.

As an example, there are fairly expensive projects by several major computing manufacturers to develop a machine which will print on both sides of a piece of paper, for the public utilities people. They are insisting that due to mailing requirements they have to print billing information on one side and your name and address on the other. There are all sorts of simple ways of doing this. For instance, there is a UNIVAC installation—pardon the horrid expression—which prints both things on one side. The continuous form goes from the printer into a device which folds it over double and laminates the backs together to give the desired two sided piece of paper. And I thought that this was a beautiful solution to the problem until I found out the cost of the special forms was four times the cost of the high speed printer rental and maintenance! So it would be a more practical solution to double the cost of the machine—have two completely separate high speed printing stations say—run some cheap paper past it, and print on both sides. Crazy? But it's a problem that will be of importance to you folks when you get sufficiently deeply into the problems of mechanical input and output of information to your document storage devices, in the distant future.

The nostrums, the hardware, even the systems that we advocate in this meeting will be as dead as mutton ten years from now. And most of you won't be; that's one of the reasons why there is still some faint value to liberal education. If we teach only handbook techniques, and I suppose there is such a thing as "handbook" literature and "handbook" library science—as a matter of fact, I think library science is cluttered with handbook art—if we teach only those things, in a rapidly moving field, what you have learned will be obsolete in a few years. If, instead, you are taught how to think, if your are taught the basic sciences, the basic languages, the basic arts of communication, you will have some value from your education still remaining ten, twenty, or even thirty years from now. And in this field especially, I very definitely envisage the fantastic advances which have taken place in the digital computing and business data handling fields in the past fifteen years. So let's keep our interests alive but at the broadest level so that when it turns out that you've backed the wrong hardware you won't be left without any valuable experience.

What we need for the distant future is two classes of machinery, an expensive and an inexpensive class. I won't attempt to define those two terms; product planning people would be down here with shotguns! But it is clear that the kinds of information retrieval which will be done for small valuable collections and for very large general collections are entirely different. Many people want to retrieve a large chunk of information, a document which contains a great deal of information. Much of the material is not specifically indicated, but in a research situation you may want to browse through the entire document to see if it produces any new ideas. A different problem is faced by intelligence officers, or by people who run telephone directories and post offices, who want to ask a single precisely stated question and come up with a single precise answer.

I used as an example the boiling point of a certain organic chemical. Well, that sounds like an example of the second type, but not necessarily. It depends on the person who asks it, and the kind of collection which the librarian in charge is supervising. If this question is being asked in an advanced research lab or a big university library, the person may want that specific piece of information only because it will lead him in new directions. He doesn't really want to know what the exact figure is. What he really wants is to open new vistas; he wants information which will lead him to ask other more rewarding questions and so on until he has something new. On the other hand, if this question arises in an organization where someone is compiling a handbook, he literally and seriously just wants that boiling point. He might like to know who said so, he might like to know how precise it was, but by and large if you tell him the answer is 364·2° centigrade, he's satisfied. He writes it down and then asks an entirely different and unrelated question.

It was, of course, the first concept that Vannevar Bush celebrated in his well-known article "As We May Think", when he talked about laying trails through a collection of information and notes. The idea was that you might trip over another man's trail and find it rewarding to follow his processes of association rather than to continue to pursue the exact fact that you were looking for when you started. But these are hard things to do. We have found in supplying computing equipment, for instance, that the last stronghold of the desk calculator, the last place where a guy wants a million dollar computer, is the research laboratory. One might think it would be exactly the other way around: first the research lab, then the engineers, and finally the finance boys.

But the research men don't have their questions sufficiently well formulated to hand them over to a professional group and say, "Here, do a great big job and come back and tell me the answers". There are, of course, exceptions. Our machines are used very effectively in nuclear research, in celestial mechanics research, in aerodynamics; without these tools progress is now almost impossible in such areas. But it was the people who had precise questions, who were not trying to find a path to new knowledge but who simply wanted specific answers—the engineering level people, the development people—who were the great proponents of computing equipment. By the same token, the information retrieval and document retrieval problems of a genuine research institution are going to be very difficult. Whether such institutions will have the initiative to solve this problem is a question. So far, if I may be blunt, and with all apologies to Dean Boaz, the universities have lagged behind industry in the subject matter we are discussing today, and the few people in industry who have been faced with big jobs of information handling have sponsored establishment of the enterprises which are trying to sell solutions to these problems.

Let's talk about the retrieval of particular documents when your descriptors are erroneous. One limitation on most of the systems currently proposed is accuracy of inquiry. Human beings correct for small errors very easily. If you type up a catalogue card and put a "p" in Smith, unless it's a Wodehouse entry nobody is particularly affected. Computing machines and their electronic friends, who I hope will work for you, are much more stubborn. That "p" is in there; in fact, that "p" is an extremely interesting artifact to a computing machine. So it concentrates on the "p". Now, this is present-state-of-the-art, and it is not satisfactory. Some of you may have seen a short excerpt from a talk I once gave for Jim Perry, which appeared in the *Saturday Review* a couple of years ago. In it I described the good human librarian in about the following terms: "You ask her for a book and you describe as being so thick, but it wasn't, it was *so* thick; you say it was orange, but it was really a shade of red; you say you took it out about three months ago, but it wasn't you, it was your office mate; you say it was published in Berlin, but it was really Leipzig; you're five years off when you guess at the publishing date; and the subject matter—yes, you're in the right ball park, but actually you said what you were interested in, and the title of the book doesn't happen to mention it specifically. And the human librarian, if she's in a collection with which she's familiar, usually goes right over to the shelf—

and finds that someone else has it out"! Now, it's going to be a tough problem to get our electronic servants to do this for us. But I honestly believe you are going to have to have this. You see, we understand pretty well how the human being does this. The librarian has been given a mass of information, most of which is erroneous, but it isn't completely erroneous. Red is closer to orange than purple, and Berlin is nearer Leipzig than Moscow or Tokyo. There is some information content in those descriptors, but there is sure a lot of error too. Now, you've got multiple descriptors. That book exists at the intersection of eight or nine items I mentioned. And there is only one book at the intersection of this fairly hazy mass. We need semantic methods, and these methods will probably have to be programed into large scale digital computers for experimental investigation first, before we try to solder them into the less expensive gadgets. We need methods that will look for the intersection of redundant descriptors, each of which is at least slightly erroneous, and some of which may be completely out of phase.

You may feel that it's going to be a long hard row to hoe. Let me close by telling you a little story about the computer business. When I busted into it, long years ago, before I had gray in my whiskers, the computing machine was considered to be pretty good. It would multiply a couple of numbers together and punch the answer out in five or six seconds. This was four or five times as fast as a clerk could do it on an electrically driven desk calculator, writing the answer down with pencil and paper. And it only cost a couple of times as much as a clerk, so we were real tickled with it. It had a big memory; as many as ten large numbers at one time could be stored away inside this machine. And it was reliable. It would do thousands of operations between mistakes, where a human being with a desk calculator could do perhaps a hundred between mistakes. So we really thought we had something. Yesterday afternoon in Kingston, New York, I walked through a computer that covered more than an acre of floor space—one of the FSQ-7 computers which are the heart of the SAGE air defense system. They're making them in mass production up there; in fact, it's harder to find the acre than it is to make the machine. I went from there to Poughkeepsie, where I was concerned with a machine a hundred times as fast as the fastest that you can buy or rent today, a machine capable of multiplying those same two numbers I talked about and recording the result, not at the rate of six hundred an hour, but at the rate of five hundred thousand per second. And that's not the end. Sure, it will be a couple of years before you'll be able to go out and rent one of these babies, and you'd better bring a barrel of money when you try. But already we are planning faster ones. Memory? This Sage computer has a new experimental memory that remembers sixty-five thousand large numbers and gets any one of them back to the central machine in six micro-seconds—six millionths of a second. That's the *little* memory! Reliable? Well, we do billions and billions of operations between errors now, although the speed has gone up so fast that the machines still only run a few hours before they break down.

Those of you who are new to this business will wonder how many decades this took. The answer is—one! I was present at Oak Ridge in the spring of 1949, less than nine years ago, when IBM delivered the very first commercial electronic business machine to the Oak Ridge Laboratories. There are two hundred of the giants out now, and more coming off as fast as we can build them. There are two thousand medium sized machines. All this happened in *one* decade. And it can happen in your field too.

I do not believe such a mass of machinery will appear, because most of the collections that are vital to our further progress are not imbedded in a sufficiently expensive matrix to warrant such a tremendous expansion. But there are cases—military intelligence, the Patent Office, valuable research collections where a single experiment repeated unnecessarily may cost tens of thousands of dollars—just aching for equipment in the hundred thousand dollar range.

They are not running around waving million-dollar bills. But on the other hand, when we started this tremendous expansion in the computer field nobody was screaming for a STRETCH or a LARC either. Your customers may very well be that demanding ten years from now.

What I want to know is, how many of you are going to be able to keep up with such an expansion? How many people in the library science field today are interested in information theory? How many are interested in the new communication and computing devices? I don't mean going out and creating them—that's not your business. But how many of you are keeping up with the field? How many of you are really reading about it? In this group the answer is probably a pretty high percent, but then you wouldn't be here today if you weren't. There are acres of the unwashed who don't come to these meetings. I want you to go back as missionaries. Tell them that we think it is about time to make a giant electronic stride in processing and retrieving information.

Information Needs of Applied Research

MERRITT L. KASTENS

Assistant Director, Stanford Research Institute
Menlo Park, California

ANYONE who has performed research or development work or has been active on the various phases of publication or library work knows that there is a problem in locating technical information. Most people with such experience agree that this problem is of major proportions.

However, there has been a tendency in some quarters in recent months to minimize both the size and the urgency of the problem. This apparent complacency may derive from failure to appreciate certain characteristics of the state of technical and scientific activity in this country and its relation to information systems. Total research activities in the United States seem to be expanding regularly about 10 per cent a year. If we are not faced with some sort of law of diminishing scientific returns, we can infer that the output of written scientific and technical information is increasing at about the same rate. Estimates of the growing volume of publication of technical articles, monographs, and research reports, as well as technical books, tend to support this inference. The primary significance of this observation lies in that the growth rate is exponential. The problem will be twice as difficult and twice as costly to solve in 1968 as it is today.

Let me remind you of another statistic. For better or for worse, some 90 per cent of the probable $7 billion that will be spent on research in this country in 1958 will be spent for applied research —research done to solve the specific practical problems of industry and of the military, and largely done in industrial laboratories or in the laboratories of applied research organizations, such as Stanford Research Institute. Remember too that industry, and to a lesser extent the government, has, in addition to its professional staffs in the research departments, at least an equal number of production engineers, operating engineers, technical market research people, and executives, who depend regularly and importantly on technical and scientific information obtained from written public media.

It is obvious that the overwhelming mass of the technical and scientific information problem is centered in the application of science and technology on various levels and that, furthermore, in the nature of our society this sort of application is carried out largely in the industrial community.

I emphasize this point with some force because it seems to have had surprisingly little attention in many of the public and semi-public discussions of the problem within the last six months. The relatively small number of productive basic scientists in any specific field seems to have little trouble in communicating among themselves, primarily because of the small number of individuals involved. If there is an immediate problem in the communication of basic science information, it is in the link between the basic scientist and the next step in the chain of technological development represented primarily by the industrial applied researcher. The possible advantages to be realized through better information exchange *between* fields of basic science is probably substantial but can only be guessed at at the present time.

It is in applied research, or programed research, activities where the technical information problem in all its complexity becomes most apparent.

A first outstanding characteristic of the information problem in the application of science is the inherent time deadline, either specified or implied. The applied researcher is always concerned with *when* he gets his information, as well as *whether* he gets it. In many cases, if he does not get what he needs in time, the information is literally of no use to him. This time consideration almost never applies to the basic or academic scientist. If he does carry out some apparently needless experimental program through lack of knowledge of similar work elsewhere, subsequent knowledge of parallel data will confirm his theoretical findings and often permit a further elaboration of the theory.

A second significant difference lies in the kind of information used by the basic and the applied scientist. The theoretical investigator, since he has personal control over the statement of his problem, tends to define his objectives in terms of certain classical or academic categories or at least to approach the problem from the exclusive point of view of such a category. Unfortunately, the practical problems which face the applied researcher do not come neatly packaged as problems in chemistry or physics or biology or electrical engineering. The solution to these practical problems may well be found through the techniques of one of the classical or academic disciplines. But even to find the proper avenue to the solution almost inevitably requires the investigation of a myriad of possible information sources in many fields and on many levels of sophistication.

Related to this problem of complexity in applied research is the episodic nature of the majority of programed research. Although the applied researcher normally stays in his chosen field of interest throughout his entire professional career, he often must shift from aspect to aspect of the problems which attract his attention. As his programs or projects modify, he is faced repeatedly with the need to familiarize himself with entire new areas of literature, either in theory, in practice, or both.

In view of these factors, it is not at all surprising that the bulk of the economic burden of the technical information processing currently falls on industrial organizations and on government agencies faced with practical technological problems. At Stanford Research Institute we have made a rough estimate that approximately 25 per cent of our professional man hours are spent in technical communications of some kind. This figure includes the time of our librarians and literature specialists. It also covers literature searches of all kinds and the time spent in keeping up with the current literature. Finally, a substantial component is represented by time spent in internal seminars and in attending technical and professional meetings for

C

verbal exchange of information. The scope of interest of our professional staff extends from psychology and sociology and economics through the various laboratory sciences to advanced engineering development. The incidence of communication effort is not evenly distributed through all kinds of activities, but it may be that our average experience is representative.

I suspect that the processing of technical information is now costing the American economy something in excess of a billion dollars a year. The majority of this cost is paid out directly by American industry. The next big contributor of course is the federal government. It would be foolhardy to attempt to predict how much saving is possible in this national function. However, the number is of such a magnitude that even a small percentage saving would represent a most impressive number of dollars.

Let me take the remainder of my time to comment on some of the major obstacles that will be faced in making a major improvement in our technical information processing capabilities. It is rapidly becoming a cliche that " The electronics people will build you an information processing machine tomorrow if somebody will tell them what the machine is supposed to do". Although this statement may not be quite literally true, it does reveal many of the profound conceptual problems involved in information processing.

First of all, taking the statement in its broadest implication, just what do we "want it to do"? What information will it process? What kind of information will it present? Whom should it be designed to serve? In what way? How much, and what kind of processing should it perform? And finally, after having answered these questions, and many more, how big will it have to be and how fast will it have to operate?

These are systems-type questions and they must be answered before there can be any sensible decision as to what "it"—the information processing machine—is to be: whether it is to be one or many, centralized or disbursed, fantastically complex or reasonably simple.

The machine designer and his colleagues, the systems designer, must have the answer to these "what" questions before they can tackle the "how" questions.

However, these "what is it supposed to do" type questions, although they can be stated separately, are not really discrete considerations. They are all interrelated and can only be attacked as a complex feedback network, or to use an increasingly popular label, a "System". It is not impossible to attack the components of this system, either conceptually or mechanically, as individual tasks. However, in the absence of what could only be called phenomenal luck, such an approach will most certainly be inefficient and might prove to be completely ineffectual.

Now I have heard it said that the really big problem in mechanizing the storage and retrieval of information is that it will involve "feeding language, which everybody knows is irrational, into machines that are inherently and inflexibly rational". This has the makings of another durable cliche. However, like many cliches, it may be true by inference, but not stand up too well under literal analysis. First of all, machines may be inherently rational, but they can be designed with a remarkable tolerance for errors, ambiguities, approximations, and just plain vagueness. More important, although everyone may be frustrated and annoyed on occasion with the inaccuracies of language, language cannot be completely irrational or it would not function at all. I will grant that we know disappointingly little about the rationale of language, but if we hope to couple this pattern which is language to the logical system of a machine, we will have to learn more about the logical framework on which language is built.

To take a readily apparent case in point—we have a number of very competent people exploring the possibilities of machine abstracting, or automatic machine encoding. Personally, I am quite optimistic about the prospects for major progress through this line of approach, and I wish there were still more people in the field. However, all this work is based on the implied, and probably fully justified assumption, that there is a statistical, which is to say a rational, relationship between word frequency, word distribution, word sequence, or some other characteristic of language, and the intellectual content of the article being processed. It would be extremely helpful if we knew a little more about the exact characteristics of this relationship. For instance, what is the "signal-to-noise" ratio in language, or perhaps equally important, what is the range of signal-to-noise ratios? Viewed as a pattern-matching problem, what is the dimensionality of the verbal description of ideas? Is it linear? Bi-dimensional? Poly-dimensional? Some of the advanced mathematical techniques should be useful in understanding these relationships, perhaps correlation theory or information theory can give us some insight. Added insight would give us much help in designing our "machine". It might tell us, if nothing else, how sensitive our system must be, and it might even lead us to the discovery of semantic filter circuits which would eliminate some of the noise by enabling us to differentiate between noise and signal.

These kinds of questions lead me to a problem which is perhaps more interesting to me as a research administrator than it is to either scientists or information specialists. I am becoming increasingly convinced that in order to advance the technology of information processing, we are going to have to make some basic discoveries. However, I am in general agreement with the cliche quoted above, that the electronic technology is ready if somebody will put it to work. I do not believe that the new discoveries are going to have to be made in machine capabilities or electronics design, although some further improvements will undoubtedly be required. I believe that our foundation in basic science is inadequate, but I think that the deficiency is in such sciences as linguistics and semantics and, quite probably, in classical logic and epistemology.

Now this factor presents a new problem. Disagreeable as it may be to some people, I am convinced that in the natural sciences we have learned to invent—or I might even go so far as to say create—on schedule. The organization of creative research effort may still be largely an art, but it is an art that is being increasingly understood and which has developed effective techniques.

I am not sure, however, that we know how to set up a research team to tackle a problem in epistemology, or in semantics. I don't know what kind of people to put on such a team, or what kind of formal training or experience or background they should have. I certainly wouldn't know how to help them design their experiments or to set up their preliminary hypotheses.

And yet, I am not at all convinced that the needed fundamental progress cannot be made and made soon enough to be useful. I am convinced that we must attempt such achievement, and I suspect that the best way to find out how to do it is to get about trying it.

In not much more than fifty years, we have learned to put the curiosity of the natural philosophers to work to solve our human problems and to satisfy many of our human desires. In perhaps the last twenty-five years we have made major strides in learning to exploit the more humanistic sciences of economics, sociology, and psychology. Logic and the more philosophical aspects of mathematics have in recent years suddenly found themselves working side by side with the disciplines of mechanical and electrical engineering in the development of complex machines systems. It would appear that now we have reached a situation in which still other areas of orderly intellectual effort can be called on to help with the work of the world.

This then brings me to what I hope is the "message" of this presentation. The relatively new ability to organize scientific effort for directed achievement has vastly increased the importance, and consequently the size, of technical activities in this country and, to a lesser extent, throughout the world. This increase has created a communications problem within the technical community which is now very large and which is increasing exponentially in size, cost, and complexity. For a number of reasons, some pertinent and some not, this problem is now rather belatedly receiving quite general consideration and may soon be the subject of a concerted technological attack.

The size and complexity of the problem appears to have disconcerted some, including a few who have in the past been most articulate in pointing out the problem. This reaction has resulted in a tendency in some circles to minimize the problem or to abandon hope of improvement in despair.

I see not need for such dismay. I have confidence in the tools, both intellectual and mechanical, which we now have at our disposal to apply to problems of high social and technological complexities, such as the one discussed here. I am also convinced that it is neither desirable nor necessary to attempt to nibble the problem to death. Delay and equivocation can only make the technical information problem more difficult and more costly. A realistic and productive program to solve the problem will require the active support of both the public and the technical and industrial communities. Persistent effort will be required to assure that what *can* be done *will* be done, and will be done at the time when it is easiest—and that time is NOW.

Linguistic Analysis in Machine-Translation Research

H. P. EDMUNDSON

The RAND Corporation
Santa Monica, California

SINCE the summer of 1956, Dr. D. G. Hays and I have been working on machine translation (MT) at The RAND Corporation. As a consultant on this project, we have been fortunate to have the services of Professor Harper, of the Slavic Language Department at UCLA. In our machine translation research Dr. Willis Ware has advised us on machines and Mr. Roy Sutton is the senior programer.

Dr. Hays and I plan to discuss two topics: we will sketch the concepts of linguistics pertinent to machine translation research, and we will briefly describe RAND's methodology for realizing machine translation. The scope of our research has been limited to English translations of Russian physics and mathematics as encountered in a typical publication like the Reports of the USSR Academy of Sciences, the *Doklady*.

To set the stage, it is necessary to make a few remarks about languages and linguistics. To a linguist, the word "language" refers principally to the spoken mode of expression. Instead, however, we are going to focus our attention on the written mode of language.

This restriction will hold throughout the sequel. The most general linguistic problem is one in which a language L_1 called the source language is to be transformed into a second language L_2 called the target language. This is diagramed in the following way: $L_1 \to L_2$; L_1 is the source language, L_2 is the target language, and T is the linguistic transformation. Since there are many types of language, they can be grouped into three convenient classes. First, we have *natural languages*, such as Russian and English. Second, we have *formal languages*, such as mathematics and logic. Third, we have *coded languages* such as binary code, decimal code, and alphabetic codes.

The ideas needed from linguistic theory go back quite a few years and have been summarized in the work of the Polish school under Ajdukiewicz (1935) and here in the United States by Zellig Harris. The first major notion is that of the *vocabulary* which is the set of all words being used in the language. This is an open-ended set in the sense that new words are being created; it is a dynamic thing. It is necessary to make the distinction immediately between two kinds of vocabularies for MT purposes. One is a *glossary*; the second is a *dictionary*. A glossary is the set of distinct running words of a corpus, or body of text, as they actually occur. On the other hand, a dictionary is an abstraction of the vocabulary. In a dictionary, not all the basic words are encountered. For example, we find the nominative singular for nouns and the infinitive for verbs.

The second major notion of linguistic theory is that of a *grammar*. Grammar as it is taught in grade school is sub-divided into two categories: morphology and syntax. *Morphology* is a description of the forms of words. *Syntax* is a description of groups of words such as phrases, clauses, and sentences. In syntax the problem of structure or composition enters for the first time.

The third major notion of linguistic theory is *semantics* which concerns the meanings of words. In translation the problem of meaning leads to the question of multiple meaning (the poly-semantic problem), and there exist several methods that can be used to attack this semantic problem. Let us now turn from linguistic theory to linguistic practice.

Machine translation can be related to a somewhat larger class of problems that we will call machine linguistics, which will be abbreviated by the symbol ML. Under this general heading, there is machine indexing MI, machine retrieval MR, machine abstracting MA, and machine translation MT. They can be characterized by describing their source language, target language, and transformation. For example, in machine indexing we pass from a natural language N to a coded language C by means of an indexing operation I: $N \xrightarrow{I} C$. In the case of machine retrieval, we do just the opposite. We go from a coded language C to a natural language N by means of a retrieval operation R: $C \xrightarrow{R} N$. This gives us the title of the document or perhaps the full text. A slightly more complex transformation is that of machine abstracting, in which we go from a natural language N to a condensed version customarily involving the same natural language N by means of an abstracting operation A: $N \xrightarrow{A} N$. In machine translation we go from one natural language N_1 to a second natural language N_2 by means of a translation operation T: $N_1 \xrightarrow{T} N_2$.

The general translation operation T encountered in MT is extremely complex, and has yet to be adequately described. Linguists and grammarians have written grammar books to this end, but at the present time only a slight dent has been made in giving a satisfactory description of this transformation that is intelligible to a machine. This, of course, is the central task that confronts us.

Let us now turn specifically to efforts to translate Russian into English. It should be clear that the complex operation T has to be factored into many simpler operations that are susceptible of description. For example, the translation of the Russian language R into the English language E, is not a one-to-one mapping in general; i.e. for one Russian word R_1 you may have two English equivalents E_1 and E_2 of which E_2 is an English equivalent for another Russian word R_2.

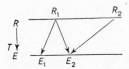

Clearly this is a rather complicated mapping. We will not discuss the inverse mapping of English to Russian since we are not concerned

with this problem in this country at the present time! Instead, let us examine the specific tasks that we have blocked out for our machine translation research.

The first task is the compilation of a *word list*. The second task is the *classification of forms*; here is meant some kind of grammar coding. We are interested not only in old classes of forms, such as parts of speech—but also in new classes that are more informative than the classical eight parts of speech. This classification depends on both the source language and the target language. The third task is the listing of *syntactic rules*. Syntactic rules are necessary to describe the structure or composition of the language. The fourth task is the listing of *semantic rules*. One of the ideas here—an old one that has come to the fore recently—is that of a thesaurus in which words are grouped by meaning, not by structure or morphological behavior. The last task is the writing of *computer routines* that combine the results of the preceding four tasks.

What are the tools available for meeting these tasks? Ultimately, these tools are mathematical, and are taken from several fields of mathematics. The first major field upon which we can rely is symbolic or deductive logic. Here we have available several different logics since there is no single logic for mathematics. The first one is the calculus of propositions. You recall that the propositional calculus deals with statements of the type "*a* or *b*", "*a* and *b*", "not *a*", and "*a* implies b". In fact, the digital computer relies on the propositional calculus in the logical portion of its program. The second one is the calculus of sets; e.g. "set *A* is included in set *B*", "sets *A* and *B* intersect", and "sets *A* and *B* do not intersect". The third logic is the calculus of relations which promises to play an increasingly important role. This can be exemplified by the relationship "father of"; e.g. *x* is the father of *y*. We are concerned also with a derived relation called the converse relation. For example, if *x* is the father of *y*, then *y* is not necessarily the son of *x*—*y* might be the daughter, so we have that *y* is the child of *x*. Similarly, a calculus of relations has been developed in which products of relations and sums of relations are defined. So much for logic, next let us turn to notions from algebra and topology.

Topology can be regarded as the branch of mathematics

concerning inter-relations of objects in terms of relative position, not in terms of absolute distance. For example, the point *x* is outside the circle; how far outside is not relevant. This is an oversimplification, but the germ of the idea. Some of the topological and algebraic objects that we can use are trees and lattices. A mathematical tree is a very simple concept—it can be drawn more easily than said.

Thus a tree is a branched structure that starts at a node and branches into several other nodes, and so forth. Trees can be used in syntactic analysis if we regard, say, the first node as the sentence *s*, which then branches into two nodes; one for the subject *n* and one for the verb *v*. If we affix these symbols to the tree you can see what is meant. We can continue this process regarding a noun phrase as a branched structure of its components by attaching the adjectives to the nouns, and so forth. A lattice is a little more complicated. Rather than define it precisely, we will imagine this tree which is spreading out at the bottom, rejoining itself, and ending up at a single node at the bottom. We then have a branched structure that is an example of a lattice.

Both trees and lattices have attracted the attention of linguists in the machine translation field.

The third major field of mathematics that provides us with tools is that of statistics and probability. One of the most important phenomena in linguistic behavior is *frequency* of occurrence. We are interested in the frequency distributions of words, pairs of words, triples of words, and more complicated strings of words. In connection with this, one of the most interesting linguistic phenomena can be approximated by an empirical law due to Zipf. The Zipf law arises in a variety of contexts, not only in written language but in spoken language, in the behavior of Chinese characters, and in the behavior of syllables. The most frequent word that occurs in text, perhaps the word "the", is ranked number one—it has rank 1. The second most frequent word to occur, perhaps the word "and", has rank 2. We would then like to relate the rank to the frequency— how frequently the word with that rank actually occurred. If r denotes the rank and f_r denotes the relative frequency of that rank, we get the following approximation in a law first stated by Zipf:

$$f_r \approx \frac{c}{r}$$

where $c = 0\cdot1$.

This interesting law states that the relative frequency of occurrence of a word which has a rank r is approximately equal to a constant $c = 0\cdot1$ divided by the rank number. Moreover, it states that this holds for each word in the text. In fact, it holds for a wide variety of linguistic phenomena. Here, then, is a fertile area for the discovery of new empirical laws involving the notions of frequency and rank.

A second major phenomenon is that of *dependency*. Using statistics and probability, we seek to discover interdependencies. One measure of the degree of dependency is the correlation coefficient. A recently completed RAND study publishes the correlation coefficients for joint pairs of occurrence of some 200 Russian words. It shows that words associate in certain classes. How and why they associate as measured by the correlation coefficients for each contingency table is under study. The preceding mathematical tools and others are available for attacking the MT problem.

Lastly, let us consider MT research methodology. The researcher has at his disposal two essentially different techniques: the theoretical and the empirical. Linguists have developed the theoretical techniques. In the meantime, however, insufficient language data has been compiled, so that empirical techniques somewhat lag behind the advanced theoretical studies that have been made for grammas and syntactics. Most of the machine translation efforts in thir country have started from the theoretical basis. Because it hadn't been tried seriously before, we decided to develop the empirical approach. Some 200,000 occurrences of Russian scientific words have been collected and their behavior studied. We are not adverse to borrowing concepts from the theoretical field, because we play one against the other. The method goes from theory to empirical results and back again. The resulting analysis provides a feedback to the theory, so the theory is modified. This is a cyclic approach to the determination of the transformation T. We write down what the operation T grossly involves, and then try a sample of text using that transformation to see what is good about T and where it fails. T is then refined and tried again on another sample of text. This cyclic approach is a means of successive approximation to the operation T. It is not to be expected that linguists can merely think long and hard about the transformation and then invent a perfect machine program the first time.

In conclusion, we note that substantial data has been collected, and rough translations have been produced on a machine. Since language data is certainly more deficient then the linguistic theory, the operation T is best approximated by means of cycling—successive refinements of the machine program. It is felt that the results obtained from machine translation research can be profitably transferred to the problems of machine indexing, machine retrieval, machine abstracting, and vice versa.

Automatic Computers in Machine-Translation Research

D. G. HAYS

The RAND Corporation,
Santa Monica, California

EVERYTHING that Dr. Edmundson has said could lead equally well into a discussion of computer problems in indexing, or retrieval, or any other field of linguistic application of the digital computer, but since we were supposed to tell you about machine translation, it's my duty now to explain how the performance of the tasks mentioned by Dr. Edmundson can lead to automatic translation from one natural language to another: from Russian to English, for example.

1. RAND'S METHOD OF RESEARCH

An automatic digital computer is nothing more nor less than a mathematical machine. It's a mechanical device for performing the simple arithmetic operations with which you are all certainly familiar—additions, subtractions, multiplications, and so forth—and some of the operations of logic that Dr. Edmundson mentioned earlier. The operations of sentential calculus, class calculus, and set theory can be performed mechanically. To put it another way, a digital computer is a very flexible device for realizing mathematical theories; a mathematical theory of language is required if we are to use the computers with language materials as inputs.

This theory must not only be "mathematical" so that the computer will operate with it, but also must be empirically based so that we can be sure the computer will operate on Russian. The theory must be internally consistent and concise, but it must also be a description of a natural language. Because of this importance of empirical exactness, as well as logical consistency, the method of research which we have developed at The RAND Corporation begins with the preparation of Russian printed textual material: for example, printed pages from the *Reports of the Academy of Sciences* and the *Journal of Experimental and Theoretical Physics*. Preparation means transforming the printed page into punched cards, punched tape, magnetic tape, or whatever material is suitable for input to the machine.

The second step is development of a word list. This word list is a glossary, since it is prepared from a specific body of text. It is an alphabetic list of all of the spelling variants—*is, are, was, were*, and not simply *be*—in the original text. To complete the glossary, we add to each Russian form an English equivalent, or several English equivalents perhaps, and some grammatic and semantic information; that is, we place each item in the glossary within a *form classification*: We apply a *grammar code*, which is the same thing, as Dr. Edmundson explained.

The third step is translation of the original Russian text. The translation is made in part by a computer, and in part by a human translator. The part that can be done by the computer depends on the refinement and sophistication of the computer program which we have available—in short, depends on our linguistic theory. The part that remains for the human translator is all that is necessary for clear and accurate translation.

The final step, which closes the circle, is empirical analysis—analysis of the translation and the original text together, looking for the clues in the original Russian version which led the translator to perform certain specific operations. Why did the translator do what he did? We attempt to remove idiosyncratic elements by having several translations made as checks on each other. The end product depends on the form of the original Russian text, and the purpose of analysis is to relate the translation to the text. From this analysis, we obtain refinements of the linguistic theory and that, in practice, means refinements of the computer program and refinements of the glossary entries.

Analysis affects the content of the glossary and the content or shape of the translation program. The entire approach is cyclic in this sense. A block of text, a corpus of about 30,000 running words or roughly one complete issue of a scientific journal, is taken as the text for a single cycle. This corpus is prepared for machine input; a glossary for that text is developed; a translation of that text is prepared; an analysis of that particular corpus is completed; the glossary is revised; the translation program is revised; and then another block of about 30,000 running words of text is entered into this process. Let me just mention a couple of numbers to show you where we stand. At the RAND Corporation we have now prepared about 100,000 running words of text, and we have obtained by a cooperative effort with a project at the University of Michigan, an equal amount again. We have made a similar cooperative agreement with Dr. D. R. Swanson of the Ramo–Wooldridge Corporation who is doing very similar work. We are arranging to make an exchange of the glossary that now stands at The RAND Corporation for some glossary that will be developed in the next few months at Ramo–Wooldridge. It will also be possible to make comparisons of the glossary we're working on with one which is being developed for a different field. We've been working with physics and mathematics; we're anxious to compare this material with a chemistry glossary, which is being developed at Georgetown University, where a substantial project is under way. I believe that we have prepared more text at this time, but current plans at the Georgetown project call for a great deal of text preparation so that we will eventually be able to compare quite sizeable physics and chemistry glossaries and perhaps give some definition to the "core language" of all science.

We have not completed treatment of our 200,000 running words of text. We have prepared glossary for about half of it; about

100,000 running words of text yielded us a glossary of about 12,000 spelling variants. We have completed the translation and analysis only for one corpus, or about 30,000 running words. Additional cycles of translation and analysis are now under way.

Perhaps I should point out that this method is not the only method that is believed to be workable, since at Georgetown University a great deal more work has gone into computer programing before their second cycle of text preparation. And at the University of Washington in Seattle, and at Harvard University, in the Computation Laboratory, dictionaries, as opposed to glossaries, are being prepared for certain fields.

2. COMPUTER NEEDS

I should say a few things about the computer requirements for this operation. At present, our text preparation, which is an input step in computer terms, is being performed by means of keypunches operated by girls who know Russian well enough to recognize characters of the alphabet. We believe that there will be character-reading or print-reading devices available within the next five years, with luck (and with urgency perhaps sooner than that), which will provide automatic input from the printed page to magnetic tapes, say. The availability of such devices will reduce the cost of the whole operation very significantly, and will probably have an enormous effect not only on machine translation but also on other areas of machine linguistics.

The glossary problem comes under the ordinary caption of storage—that is, a large capacity, high-speed storage device is needed. At present, we're using punched cards, which have infinitely large capacity if you like, but very low access speed. A high-speed, high-capacity storage device is needed in the long run, and in fact there are such devices under development now. For example, a device was developed at International Telemeter under an Air Force contract; we hope to see that device completed very soon. Another device is under development at Bell Telephone Laboratories for use in Bell's new or proposed electronic central offices. Such a device will most likely be available in the size and speed needed in five years or less.

For translation, computational ability is needed, but we have a great deal of that today. The operations of translation are no different from the operations of any other kind of computation; however, it may well be that special purpose devices, special purpose computers, would be more economical, or more easily tailored to the programs which combine operations and perform the translation task. It may be that input and storage devices are available at such high speed that a faster computer is needed to keep up with them.

Finally, the translation must be printed out. For this output, a special purpose piece of hardware that could print out mathematical equations, chemical formulas and so forth would be eminently desirable for production line translation.

It's not our feeling that we will do a certain amount of research, lick this problem, and then cut off, letting somebody else pick it up cold to do production operation. In fact, one of the merits that we see in this cyclic approach is that there is no sharp line between research and production. As each cycle is completed, there's a very strong presumption that you will find smaller and smaller increases in glossary size and smaller changes in the computer program. As the amount of glossary increases and the complexity of program change diminishes, you gradually come to say "We're doing machine translation on a production basis." The question is: how much work has to be done by human intervention in the glossary development stage, how much work has to be done by a post-editor in the translation stage? We're doing machine translation at RAND, but we're doing so much post-editing that it's far more expensive to do it our way than purely by hand. We believe that there will be a change in this balance in the near future.

3. PROGRAMING METHODS

I would like to show you specifically how the form classification or grammar code that comes from the glossary and the syntactic rules together make possible the mechanical analysis of sentence structure. This is the key step in MT, since if you can analyze the structure of a sentence in Russian, you can construct a sentence representing this structure in English.

The sentence I have in mind is:

"The electron beam impinges on the grid."

I am now going to write grammar code symbols, or form class names, below. The code symbols that I am going to use are not from a set that is sufficient for translating or analyzing English, but they're simple to work with. I'm going to say *t* for an article, *a* for an adjective, *n* for a noun, *p* for a preposition, *v* for a verb. Now the sentence reads:

The electron beam impinges on the grid.

$$t \qquad a \qquad n \qquad v \qquad p \quad t \quad n$$

The computer operates on this string of symbols, not on the original words. The symbols are obtained from a glossary, and the syntactic rules are couched in these terms.

The rules are of the form: an adjective plus a noun is the same as a noun. Applying that rule once in this sentence, I find that the sequence "electron beam", adjective-noun, is the same as a noun. The sentence isn't structurally changed much if I say, "The beam impinges on the grid". The next rule is article plus noun is equivalent to noun. The next rule may surprise you a little—it's preposition plus noun equals modifier, of a general type which I will call *d*. I say that it may surprise you because it's the first time that I've changed symbols; previously, the name of the phrase was the same as the name of the one of its members. Now I have a rule which says that a verb followed by a modifier is equivalent to a verb. Finally, a noun followed by a verb is equivalent to a sentence.

The electron beam impinges on the grid.

$$
\begin{array}{ccccccc}
t & a & n & v & p & t & n \\
\end{array}
$$

t	a	n	v	p	t	n
		n				n
	n				d	
				v		
			s			

Now suppose that I want to translate this sentence into another language. I know that this is a complete sentence; looking only at the lowest level, I see that it's composed of a noun followed by a verb. In a really complete analysis, I would know that this noun is what is called a subject. In the language to which I am translating there is a rule which says either that the noun precedes the verb or that the verb precedes the noun. It doesn't matter as long as I can write down one of those rules, so that when I find a sentence composed of noun-followed-by-verb I know in which order to place these elements in the output. I would also know if I were translating into Latin, say, what case ending was required for a noun subject and what tense, person and number endings were required for the verb. Translating from Russian to English is simpler because the case endings help me to refine the grammar code and make the rules much simpler than they are in English. Furthermore, when I get to English I don't have to worry about adding suffixes. (You will find careful treatments of the problem of adding Russian suffixes depending upon English context in certain Russian linguistic journals.)

This is the type of operation which makes possible the structural analysis of a sentence. It is an example of the type of mathematics which Dr. Edmundson referred to as the calculus of relations. The relation in the original sentence is that of succession—one word comes after another. There are certain sequences of form-classes in Russian which can be mapped into phrase names—an adjective followed by a noun depends on, or modifies, the noun and that is another of these mathematical relations. It makes no difference which of these two slightly varying descriptions you make; if an adjective modifies a noun, or if an adjective plus a noun form a noun phrase, you can translate the adjective and noun. This is an important point which we are concerned with proving purely and explicitly. It's one of the interesting questions at a theoretical level.

I'd like to say in conclusion that this kind of analysis, very familiar to linguists and to teachers of English and other languages, is what's required to make a computer analyze linguistic materials. Still lacking is a full knowledge of how many grammatic code types, how many form-classes, are necessary and what rules are required. This is what we mean by the necessity for thorough, empirical investigation of languages.

44

Auto-Encoding of Documents for Information Retrieval Systems

H. P. LUHN

IBM Research Center
Yorktown Heights, New York

INTRODUCTION

IT HAS been typical of information retrieval systems of the past that the organization of literature to facilitate its recall is dependent on human effort. Each new document that is added to a library has to be subjected to human scrutiny for assigning such tags as will permit recovery in answer to a given inquiry.

While significant progress has been made in the mechanization of information retrieval it has been limited to the acceleration of data processing. The origination of the data being processed has substantially remained an intellectual effort. Since it is apparent that the growth of literature is proceeding at an exponential rate, it becomes doubtful whether the increasing demands for human effort can be satisfied in the future. It is therefore important that means be found which will make it possible to extend machine procedures to the generation of the data itself, that is to the encoding process presently performed by humans. This means that future systems must be capable of accepting documents in their original form and of deriving from them, without human intervention, such data as

45

will subsequently permit automatic retrieval in response to a given inquiry.

A great deal of progress has been made recently in the application of statistical methods for analyzing documents by machine and for extracting from them significant elements which have properties similar to the ones formerly derived by intellectual processes. The automatic creation of literature abstracts is a good example of the feasibility of these new statistical methods.

This paper describes methods of *auto-encoding* based on statistical procedures performed by machine on the original text of a document. It is a prerequisite that such text be available in *machine-readable* form such as punched cards or tape or magnetic tape. Such machinable records are presently available to a limited extent from Teletypewriters, Flexowriters, Teletypesetters and Monotype machines. The utility of automatic literature processing systems will promote the automatic creation of machine-readable records as by-products of typing operations in the future, while the creation of machine records of existing literature would eventually be assigned to automatic print-reading devices.

DOCUMENT RETRIEVAL PATTERNS

By way of introduction to the principles of the automatic encoding process, some aspects of manual encoding will first be reviewed.

The assignment of class designations or subject headings to given documents is an intellectual process based on general familiarity with the subject matter treated in such documents. By perusing the text the indexer deduces certain characteristics and anticipates situations under which these characteristics might be of value to a potential inquirer. In this task the indexer is substantially guided by what has been typical of past motivations for inquiry. This gauging of new documents by standards of the past introduces a lag which interferes with the recognition of pertinent information in the light of new interests.

It has been the objective of more recent indexing systems to overcome this defect by avoiding classification based on past experience and instead to characterize documents by elements inherent to the documents proper. This is substantially achieved by introducing

46

classifications on the word level rather than on the sentence level or the level of categories of contents. The introduction of discriminating terms, such as key words, has brought about a new degree of freedom. Instead of applying a static set of categories or subject headings beforehand, such categories or subject headings may be formulated dynamically at the instant of inquiry by a tailor-made assembly of such key words. Subsequently the coincidence of the given key words, when present in the characterization of a document, is taken as an indication of relevance of subject matter.

The process of selecting key words makes lesser demands on the indexer than does the assignment of categories or subject headings. This simplification might therefore be considered significant as a step toward a fully mechanical solution of the document encoding procedure.

STATISTICAL METHODS OF ENCODING

Of various automatic procedures for deriving typical patterns for characterizing documents, the systems here proposed are based on operations involving statistical properties of words. The methods are based on the same arguments which have been advanced in connection with auto-Abstracting*. It is held that the more often a certain word appears in a document the more it becomes representative of the subject matter treated by the author. In grading words in accordance with the frequency of usage within a document, a pattern is derived which is typical of that document and unique amongst all similarly derived patterns of a collection of documents. It is proposed that the more similar two such patterns are the more similar is the intellectual contents of the documents they represent.

The extent to which such word-frequency lists have to be carried depends on the number of documents in a collection and on the overall degree of similarity of topic. The smaller and the more diversified the collection, the shorter need be the word list to permit discrimination amongst the documents.

The discriminatory quality here sought does not reside in such

* H. P. LUHN, "The Automatic Creation of Literature Abstracts", *IBM Journal of Research and Development*, Vol. 2, No. 2, 159–165 (April 1958).

words as articles, conjunctions, prepositions and kindred "common" words, even though they might rank high in frequency. It is therefore necessary to disregard these words. A further requirement is the consolidation of varying forms of the same word stem. For procedures involved in the elimination of common words and in word consolidation, the reader is referred to the paper on auto-abstracting.

While auto-encoding is substantially an extension of auto-abstracting, there is a condition here which calls for special attention. This is the variation of word usage amongst different authors. The means by which this condition is overcome consist of a thesaurus similar in make-up to *Roget's Thesaurus*. However, such a thesaurus serves not only to tag words of similar meaning but also to broaden the concepts of the words used. This function as well as the procedures for constructing special thesauri have been discussed in detail in an earlier paper*.

AUTOMATIC PROCEDURES OF ENCODING

The procedures involved in auto-encoding will be described in connection with a sample document (Fig. 1) consisting of a short article on a medical subject. It is assumed that a machine-readable record of the text is available. It is also assumed that a list of "common" words as well as a special thesaurus have been compiled and are available for mechanical look-up by the data processing machine employed for the task.

The machine-readable record is introduced into the machine and a word list is assembled in alphabetic order. Various forms of the same word stem are then consolidated. At the same time each word is looked up in the common word list and, if found to be a member of this list, is eliminated. The result of these operations is a word frequency list in descending order as shown in Fig. 2.

Inspection of the list will reveal that the high frequency words encompass the topic of the document more adequately than do the low frequency words. The first dozen or two dozen words disclose to a high degree what the document is about. If a similarly constructed

---

* H. P. LUHN, "A Statistical Approach to Mechanized Encoding and Searching of Literary Information", *IBM Journal of Research and Development*, Vol. 1, No. 4, October 1957.

SAMPLE DOCUMENT

The auto-encoding of this document is illustrated by way of some of the steps involved in the process. An auto-abstract of the document is also given as a matter of interest.

Experiments Suggest a New Approach to
The Treatment of Heart Attacks

By ROBERT K. PLUMB

Heart attacks, one of the most dreaded of the diseases of modern life, do not happen to women before the menopause or change of life as often as they happen to young men. Why? Do female hormones have a protective effect? Or is the different heart-attack rate among young men and young women due to some anatomic or emotional factor that medicine cannot capitalize upon? If hormones largely make the difference, possible means of using female hormones to treat men was suggested last week.

Atherosclerosis, the main cause of heart attacks, is a narrowing of the arteries by deposits made up largely of a fatty material called cholesterol. This is a constituent of many common foods and normal bodily material manufactured by a healthy liver. Links between diet, the presence of cholesterol in the blood, the development of atherosclerosis, and the occurrence of a coronary thrombosis (clot) which may shut off blood supply and damage the heart muscle (myocardial infarction) have been suggested but not established.

Action by Hormones

In the journal Endocrinology last week, researchers from the New England Institute for Medical Research in Ridgefield, Conn., reported animal tests which suggest that an important body scavenging system (the reticuloendothelial system or RES) may in animals be stimulated by female hormones possibly to remove cholesterol-like substances from the blood. The group furthermore reported on animal studies which suggest that female hormones which work best in stimulating the RES may be slightly altered so that they do not (in animals) have their powerful feminizing effects.

The report was prepared by four physicians, Dr. John H. Heller, Dr.

R. M. Meier, Dr. R. A. Zucker and Dr. G. W. Mast, all working at the non-profit medical institute founded in Ridgefield in 1954.

The studies, although they were done on laboratory animals, have great possible application in the future treatment of victims of heart attacks and other major afflictions of the arteries, Dr. Heller believes.

Many physicians have suspected that the abnormal cholesterol levels in the blood are related to heart attacks and that cholesterol levels might be lowered by administration of female sex hormones. A number of hospitals have given massive doses of female sex hormones to men. But, according to Dr. Heller, "although it was the consensus that this was successful therapy, the men developed enlarged breasts and other secondary female sexual characteristics. Such results precluded continuation of the therapy."

Sex Effect Reduced

According to the report the RES stimulatory effect of a wide variety of female hormones was measured in laboratory animals. Then new hormone-like compounds were produced which had a markedly reduced effect on sex characteristics but which maintained their stimulatory activity upon the RES. The studies established that sex effects of female hormones and the effects of male hormones in increasing the effectiveness and rapidity of the RES ability to remove injected colloids (believed to be analogous to cholesterol) could be separated. The result is a lead, at least, toward the discovery of compounds that will act like female hormones in lowering the blood cholesterol levels in ailing male heart-attack patients without the feminizing side effects.

The possible application of this finding in a practical way in the treatment of ailing men remains to be seen. There are many gaps in knowledge about atherosclerosis and heart and artery diseases. Laboratory experiments on animals, medical scientists often caution, are a long way from treatment in hospital or home.

However, Dr. Heller, the executive director of the New England Institute for Medical Research and a former member of the Biophysics Division of Yale University, believes that the experiments prove something vital: that modern medical science needs institutions in which many disciplines—such as biology, physics, internal medicine, chemistry, mathematics and electronics—can be brought to bear upon specific problems.

In the case of the experiments which lead to information about the structure of female sex hormones, Dr. Heller states, specialists who practice theoretical medicine akin to theoretical physics—are essential.

"First, the measurement of function of the RES is not easy," Dr. Heller said. "This methodology had to be developed and it required a knowledge of colloid chemistry. For instance, it was necessary to create particles (literally smaller than those particles in a puff of smoke) whose surface had to be treated to give them a negative electrical charge after they had been injected intravenously.

"One of the colloids is carbon. Procedures to make a carbon colloid to meet these specifications of purity, size and charge, demand much in the field of solid state physics and physical chemistry.

"To prove that these particles all go to the RES and not elsewhere, we had to make the particles radioactive [enter nuclear physics and radiobiology] and we had to rely upon the techniques of microradioautography."

Auto-Abstract: The result is a lead, at least, toward the discovery of compounds that will act like female hormones in lowering the blood cholesterol levels in ailing male heart-attack patients without the feminizing side effects.

* Reproduced by permission of the *New York Times*. Date of publication: September 22, 1957.

Fig. I

WORD FREQUENCY LIST

Title: Experiments suggest a New Approach to the Treatment
of Heart Attack
by ROBERT K. PLUMB

14 hormones	4 colloid	2 action	2 material
11 female	4 experiment	2 ailing	2 measured
8 effect	4 particles	2 application	2 modern
7 heart	4 possible	2 carbon	2 practice
7 animal	4 report	2 characteristics	2 prove
7 cholesterol	4 stimulated	2 charge	2 reduced
7 physics	3 artery	2 compounds	2 remove
7 RES	3 atherosclerosis	2 different	2 result
6 medical	3 believed	2 disease	2 specific
6 men	3 chemistry	2 established	2 state
6 sex	3 developed	2 feminizing	2 system
6 treatment	3 laboratory	2 heart-attack	2 theoretical
5 attacks	3 levels	2 hospital	2 therapy
5 blood	3 studies	2 injected	2 week
5 Dr. Heller	3 young	2 institute	2 women
5 suggest		2 knowledge	2 work
		2 lead	
		2 lowered	
		2 life	1 (not listed)
		2 main	

First order significant words = frequencies of 5 and over
Second order significant words = frequencies of 2, 3 and 4

Fig. 2

50

list of another document would contain a reasonably large fraction of these same words, the probability is great that the authors of the two documents talk about similar things. It is true that no direct clues are given of the specific relationships established by the authors between the words listed. It is also true, however, that only a limited number of meaningful and reasonable relationships can be synthetized. The probability that the two authors did in fact establish similar relationships between given words is therefore comparatively great.

1. *One-dimensional patterns*

Based on the foregoing arguments, the creation of an encoding pattern may consist of listing an appropriate portion of the words ranking highest on the word frequency list derived from a document. Experiments conducted so far on documents ranging in size from 500 to 5000 words have indicated that word patterns consisting of from ten to twenty-four of the highest ranking words furnish adequate discrimination and resolution for retrieval, sixteen such words being a likely average. The size of the document collection for which this size pattern will suffice has not as yet been determined. Indications are, however, that size of collection is not a major function in determining optimum pattern size.

The next step in the automatic procedure in creating a one-dimensional pattern consisting of a list of highest ranking words is the normalization of the list by look-up in the special thesaurus. The size of the list is in this case determined by the frequency step below the sixteenth word of the list so that all words of frequency 5 and above are involved. The result of the look-up is a sequence of notions as categorized by the following designations of notional families of the thesaurus (an excerpt of which is given in Fig. 4): 075, 154, 162, 315, 366, 373, 374, 514, 662, B01, C01, C02, C03, E01. This notation is given in a fixed order to facilitate searching operations. It will be noticed that the words "medical" and "treatment" have been merged in that they are members of the same notional family. The word *Dr. Heller* may be added to the list either as is or in appropriate code. This completes the automatic creation of one form of one-dimensional document pattern of the sample text.

Depending on more specific requirements of an information retrieval system other terms may be automatically added to the notation such as capitalized words irrespective of their frequency of occurrence. Furthermore, just as common words have been eliminated by look-up in a special index, certain essential words may be looked-up in another special index for the purpose of listing them under any circumstances.

2. *Multi-dimensional Patterns*

The degree of relationship expressed by one-dimensional patterns may not be sufficient in certain applications. In such cases multidimensional patterns will permit recognition of the degree to which an author has associated certain words. A first degree of association may be considered to be the immediate physical proximity of a pair of words of given significance, disregarding certain intervening words of the common word list such as: of, by, on, in, to, the, a, this, etc. Since certain words of such pairs may in turn be found to be paired with other words or word pairs, these overall relationships may be viewed as branched structures and the principles of the *Nodal index for branched structures** be applied to the development of an encoding scheme for verbal information.

Such a system would best be arranged by assigning the status of *nodes* to words of a first order set composed of highest ranking words such as selected for the one-dimensional pattern previously described. While a nodal index may be developed at the level of this selection, the system will be described here on a level which includes a second order set of words, in this case a predetermined range of frequencies adjacent to the range of the first set (first order significant words), namely, the words of frequency 2, 3, and 4 (second order significant words).

The automatic process would proceed to extract from the sentences all word pairs consisting either of two adjoining first order words or of a first order word coupled to a second order word. The result is a listing, stored in the machine, as shown in Fig. 3. As before, the

---

* H. P. LUHN, "A Serial Notation for Describing the Topology of Multidimensional Branched Structures (Nodal Index for Branched Structures)," IBM Research Center, Research Report RC–27, December 1955.

LIST OF PAIRED WORDS

Word pairs are listed as they appear in the text. A pair consists either of two adjoining first order words or of a first order word coupled to a second order word. Certain intervening words are disregarded such as: of, by, on, in, to, the, a, this, that, which, like, and, or, be, was, etc.

First order words have been underlined for purposes of distinction only.

treatment heart attack

heart attack

young men

female hormones

young men

female hormones treat men suggested

heart attack

cholesterol blood developed

action hormones

reported animal

system RES animals stimulated female
    hormones possibly

remove cholesterol-like

reported animal studies

suggest female hormones work

stimulating RES

feminizing effects

medical institute

laboratory animals

heart attack

Heller believes

cholesterol levels blood

heart attacks cholesterol levels

female sex hormones

female sex hormones men

according Heller

therapy men developed

sex effect reduced

report RES stimulatory effect

female hormones measured

laboratory animals

hormone-like compounds

reduced effect sex characteristics

activity RES

established sex effects female hormones
    effects hormones

female hormones lowering blood
    cholesterol levels

feminizing effects

treatment ailing men

atherosclerosis heart artery

experiments animals medical

treatment hospital

modern medical

medicine chemistry

female sex hormones

Heller states

theoretical medicine

theoretical physics

state physical chemistry

particles RES

Fig. 3

53

THESAURUS

Listing of thesaurus index items corresponding to the words occurring in the list of paired words.

according 467
action 170
ailing 655
animal 366
artery C04
atherosclerosis A01
attack 315

believe 484
blood C02

characteristics 015
chemistry 357
cholesterol B01
compound 041

develop 161

effect 154
establish 478
experiment 463

female 374
feminizing 374

heart C01
hormones E01
hospital 662

institute 542

laboratory 691
level 026
lowering 036

measure 466
medical 662
men 373
modern 123

particle 032
physics 316
possibly 470

reduce 036
remove 301
report 527
RES C03

sex 075
state 007, 535
stimulate 171
study 461
suggest 514
system 060

theoretical 514
therapy 662
treatment 662

work 170

young 127

Fig. 4

TABLE OF WORD PAIRS

ordered according to thesaurus family number

Nodes	Branches
075 (sex)	154 (effect), 374 (female), E01 (hormones)
154 (effect)	036 (reduce), 075 (sex), 171 (stimulate), 374 (female), 374 (feminizing), E01 (hormones)
315 (attack)	B01 (cholesterol), C01 (heart)
316 (physics)	007 (state), 357 (chemistry), 514 (theoretical), 535 (state)
366 (animal)	171 (stimulate), 527 (report), 662 (medical), 691 (laboratory), C03 (RES)
373 (men)	127 (young), 161 (develop), 514 (suggest), 655 (ailing), 662 (treatment), E01 (hormones)
374 (female)	075 (sex), 154 (effect), 171 (stimulate), 514 (suggest), E01 (hormones)
514 (suggest)	373 (men), 374 (female)
662 (medical)	357 (chemistry), 366 (animal), 514 (theoretical)
662 (treatment)	373 (men), 655 (ailing), C01 (heart), E01 (hormones)
B01 (cholesterol)	026 (level), 315 (attack), C02 (blood)
C01 (heart)	315 (attack), 662 (treatment)
C02 (blood)	026 (level), 036 (lowering), 161 (develop), B01 (cholesterol)
C03 (RES)	170 (action), 171 (stimulate), 366 (animal), 527 (report)
E01 (hormones)	036 (lowering), 075 (sex), 154 (effect), 170 (action), 373 (men), 374 (female), 662 (treatment)
HELR (Heller)	007, 535 (state)

Document Pattern

Nodal Index:

075–154/374/E01, 154–036/075/171/374/E01, 315–B01/C01, 316–007/357/514/535, 366–171/527/662/691/C03, 373–127/161/514/655/662/E01, 374–075/154/171/514/E01, 514–373/374, 662–357/366/514, 662–373/655/C01/E01, B01–026/315/C02, C01–315/662, C02–026/036/161/B01, C03–170/171/366/527, E01–036/075/154/170/373/374/662, HELR–007/535.

Fig. 5

LATTICE OF WORD-PAIR LINKAGES

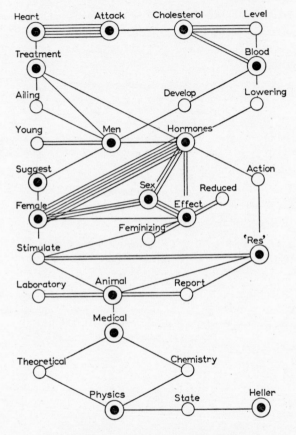

Nodes designate word frequency as follows:
1st order ◉ = 5 and over; 2nd order ○ = 2, 3, 4
Frequency of word pairs is indicated by number of intervening links

Fig. 6

words are looked up in the thesaurus and the corresponding family numbers are substituted for the words; at the same time all first order words are marked by an appropriate sign.

A record is then developed, giving for each first order word (node) all the words which have been found paired to it (branches). This information is shown in tabular form in Fig. 5 with the actual words given in parentheses for the purpose of explanation. The final serial form of the notation as shown below the table is then stored appropriately on cards, punched or magnetic tape, or the like.

This completes the automatic encoding process by way of a multidimensional pattern. There are many variations of this process which will accommodate the requirements of given situations. Again, as previously pointed out, certain special sets of words may be given a preferential status so that they would become part of the notation.

The relationships expressed by the final notation have been translated into a corresponding *lattice of word-pair linkages*, shown in Fig. 6. This diagram, based on words which were found to be paired at least twice, might serve to support the practicability of the statistical processes here proposed. It might also serve to investigate, for instance, what the effect would have been if words of frequency 2 had been excluded. It might also be interesting to observe that only a fraction of the second order words were found paired to the first order words and that this fraction comprises about the same number of different words as are contained in the list of first order words.

CONCLUSION

The systems of auto-encoding described above are representative of what may be accomplished through statistical methods in the area of information dissemination and retrieval. It is only due to the speeds and logical capabilities of electronic machines that such methods become practical in the first place and no sane person would recommend that such extensive operations be applied manually.

A great deal of research and experimentation remains to be done before characteristics of human behavior, as manifested in writing, are better understood and can be effectively utilized to improve processes of the kind here described.

The effectiveness of thesauri in overcoming variations in word usage, including foreign languages, cannot be proven until retrieval installations of substantial size have been operated for a considerable period of time.

While much remains to be done, there is the encouraging fact that research and experimentation in the areas here referred to is going on in many places within the United States and abroad and at an ever-increasing rate. It may therefore be hoped that the days of effective and economical automation of information dissemination and retrieval are close at hand.

Application of High-Speed Computers to Information Retrieval

DON D. ANDREWS

Director, Research & Development
U.S. Patent Office, Washington, D.C.

ELECTRONIC computers are exceedingly versatile tools for, in general, any manipuation of data for which the complete logic can be stated may be performed by the computer.

Since the information content of any document apparently may be symbolized by some possible set of data, it is equally apparent that an electronic computer could be used to retrieve documents having a desired prescribed informational content. The only problem is to correlate the best of the infinite number of possible ways of symbolizing the data with the best of an infinite number of ways of instructing the computer to yield the best possible information for the purpose at hand.

This can be a tremendously difficult job at our present state of knowledge. Few people have thought through the intricacies of their own information problem so as to be able to state their problems in precise logical fashion. Most people will be unable to state both the breadth and the depth of their problem.

All that we can do today is to postulate one or more modes of symbolizing our data, instruct the computer to manipulate that data and then see how near this comes to our actual information needs, which we probably don't fully understand in the first place.

Whether a computer will be an economical retrieval tool will depend upon the qualitative and quantitative needs of the user of the information. The fact that a computer may be used does not indicate that it should be used. If a simple index or a notched or punched card system meets these needs the computer is not likely to be an answer. When the resolving or discriminating power of a simple retrieval system becomes inadequate due to a high density of closely related documents as well as a wide spread of the subject matter covered by the file of documents, then a computer should be considered as a possible solution to the qualitative needs. If otherwise satisfactory devices are too slow in processing the whole file or if the traffic in the use of the system produces intolerable delays then a computer may satisfy the quantitative needs of the user. The high cost of electronic computers invites careful consideration of the economic values received against the cost incurred.

In deciding the overall needs of the information retrieval system one should realize that such systems may be basically different although there is a hope that some day we shall discover the basic theory underlying them all.

In general, there are three different types of retrieval systems with which I am familiar. Undoubtedly others will be developed.

You are probably familiar with the "statistical" method of retrieving information, although possibly not by that name.

The statistical method involves breaking down or "fragmenting" a document into a series of terms or descriptors. A collection or "set" of such terms which are descriptively applicable to a given document is assumed to symbolize that document for retrieval purposes.

The operation of retrieval with such a system consists in asking for a set of such terms or descriptors to be included within any set of terms or descriptors which has previously been applied to any single document of the collection and accepting as an answer any such document which includes within its file the complete set of preselected terms. Sometimes a lesser number than the complete wanted set may be acceptable as a satisfactory approximation of that which is really needed.

These systems of retrieval are considered to be of a "statistical" nature since they are predicated upon the probability that a match of or inclusion within two or more sets of terms or descriptors will indicate that the meaning associated with each set will be the same in spite of the fact that other terms or descriptors may also be included. Unfortunately, this is not necessarily a valid assumption, for the presence of other terms which are associated with the document but are not within the question set of terms may cause retrieval of a document wherein these terms have a meaning entirely different from that referred to by the partial set of terms.

However, if the needs of the user of such a statistical system may tolerate the amount of "noise" or false selections that is inherent in such a system due to the "crosstalk" between terms applicable to different parts of the same document and the resultant false combinations of terms, this system is extremely simple and can be very effective.

The second classification of retrieval systems is one which we shall call the "syntactical" systems. Here again, the document will be fragmented into those terms or descriptors which constitute the building blocks of which the total essential meaning of a document is constructed. But instead of these terms constituting a single set for each document as is the case of a "statistical" system, the terms are apportioned into a number of such sets or subsets. This subdivision serves to lessen "crosstalk" at least to the extent that the terms of one subset may not be unintentionally associated with terms of another subset. The subdivision within the file is maintained by a distinctive mark or signal interspersed between the respective subsets. Since these marks may have distinctive characteristics, it is possible to record information at different levels of meaning. This has been considered analogous to the spaces and punctuation marks of textual material. That is, certain terms may be grouped together to form a phrase, the phrases to form sentences, the sentences to form paragraphs and so on to even larger units. This device serves very much the same purpose as parentheses and brackets serve in mathematical expressions or formulae.

The third category of information retrieval system is one which we in the Patent Office refer to either as an "interrelational" or as a "precise" system. This latter term is not well chosen, for that which is precise and sharp by today's standards may be very elementary and blunt by tomorrow. The "interrelational" system also has the appropriate terms and descriptors of a document fragmented into groups and recorded in the fashion of the "syntactical" system but will have recorded in the file, in addition to the grouping marks or signals, the symbols which indicate the relational concepts which interconnect the various terms or blocks of the recorded data.

A model may illustrate the distinction between these three systems. Let us assume a document discloses four blocks of information which we can identify as having terms or descriptors A, B, C, and D, respectively. Let us further assume that certain relationships between these terms are specified in the document to the effect that A and B have this relationship and B also has this relationship to both C and D but C and D are not related to each other in this fashion. The document may likewise relate E and F together. This may be diagramed with the relationships being shown as interconnecting lines as follows:

$$A-B{<}^{C}_{D} \qquad E-F$$

In a "statistical" system A, B, C, D, E, and F would be recorded in our file to represent this document. Since no relationships were recorded, a request for C wanted in relationship to D must necessarily retrieve this document in spite of its nonpertinency. Likewise this document would be retrieved if the request were for D in the specified relation to E and would be equally spurious.

In a "syntactical" system since A, B, C, and D form one subset of terms and E and F form a second subset, there would be no crosstalk in the case of an inquiry addressed to the file for the terms D and E in the specified relation but the C related to D inquiry would still be erroneously retrieved.

In the "interrelational" system the retrieval can be made more commensurate with the inquiry propounded to the retrieval system by the following device. Each term that is related to any other term or terms is augmented with an arbitrarily assigned relationship number which same number is also added to any other term with which the first term is related. In the Patent Office this number is called an "interfix". Thus in the model proposed the file would appear as follows:

$$A_1$$
$$B_{1,\ 2,\ 3}$$
$$C_2$$
$$D_3$$
$$E_4$$
$$F_4$$

It is obvious that an inquiry for terms C and D in the specified relationship would properly exclude this document because no relationship number for C matches a relationship number for D. Likewise, there will be no "crosstalk" between terms D and E.

This "interrelational" system can be used in a variety of ways. It can be used on the Patent Office machine called ILAS*. Another such use is for searching chemical structural formulae by means of an electronic computer. In the Patent Office a notation system was developed in which each of the terms represented a chemical element and the relationships were the valence bond connections among the various chemical elements. Mr. L. C. Ray of the National Bureau of Standards programed SEAC, the NBS electronic computer, to make an element by element topological search through an encoded file of complex chemical compounds. In this program, the computer could recognize in its file not only the presence of each of the chemical elements and the number required of each but also the interconnections that must be present for each element†. This the computer could do irrespective of possible different orientations and mirror-image configurations between the data in the computer's file and that contemplated at the time of making the inquiry. The results achieved were very flexible since one could ask for any fragment of a chemical structure and the machine would search its entire field of information. If the set of elements specified in the question were

---

* Don D. ANDREWS, *Interrelated Logic Accumulating Scanner* (*ILAS*). Patent Office Research and Development Report No. 6. Washington 25, D.C., Department of Commerce, 1956.

† Louis C. RAY and RUSSELL A. KIRSCH, "Finding Chemical Records by Digital Computers". *Science*, **126**, 3278 (October 25, 1957), 814–819.

related exactly as had been specified anywhere within any of the chemical structures, the machine would accept this as an answer and print out the identification of the document in which this structure was disclosed.

While the processing of complex chemical structures on an element by element basis was comparatively slow, the use of larger building blocks than the chemical elements themselves, such as ring structures and functional groups, would greatly increase this speed. This would be a compromise between the present element building block and the much larger structural configurations used by Drs. Norton and Opler of the Dow Chemical Co. in their work with topological search systems for chemical structures*.

The Patent Office is now working on a new computer program which is named HAYSTAQ†. In this program not only may questions be phrased in the alternative, that is find either A or B associated with C, but also certain information concerning the chemical process involving the specified compound, such as, the compound being either a starting material, intermediate, or final product of a specified process, will be available.

The HAYSTAQ program is itself a research project since the final product of that work it is hoped will serve to delineate what the ultimate solution of the information problem might be, both intellectual and machinewise, rather than how to make a computer execute a complex empirical routine. Accordingly, the HAYSTAQ program is aimed at four different but closely related problems.

What normally would be the first problem but which has been deferred to a later time in order to get into the heart of the information problem is the pre-editing routines for data that are to be searched by the computer. This is indeed a serious problem for the burden of converting large volumes of data contained on the printed page into a form acceptable to the computer by human intellect may constitute a serious economic block to further progress.

---

* ASCHER OPLER and TED R. NORTON, "New Speed to Structural Searches." *Chemical & Engineering News*, **34**, 23 (June 4, 1956), 2812–2816.

† HAROLD PFEFFER, HERBERT R. KOLLER and ETHEL C. MARDEN, *A First Approach to Patent Searching Procedures on Standards Electronic Automatic Computer (SEAC)*. Patent Office Research and Development Report No. 10. Washington 25, D.C., Department of Commerce, 1958.

The second problem is that of pre-editing the questions which are to be processed by the computer. Obviously, data which serves to instruct a computer to perform a specific search operation must be in a highly styled format and must precisely define the actual information sought. This data may be generated by the computer itself from information in a form more conveniently composed by humans.

The third and most difficult problem is the actual searching procedure and is the one into which the Patent Office is putting its greatest effort. In general the search routine might be as follows: Units of technical information found in each document in the search file will be stored in coded form in one part of the computer's memory and corresponding information units which collectively make up the subject matter content of a single question will be stored in coded form in another part of the memory. The program now being written is contained in still another section of the memory and will cause the computer to make a series of intercomparisons between the code representing the first information unit of the question set and each of the codes representing the information units of a single document. If the computer fails to find the first question code anywhere within the codes for the first document the search of that document ceases and the codes for the next document are investigated. If the first question code is satisfied then the computer will re-investigate the same codes for the second part of the question and so on until computer satisfies itself that this document either has or has not the proper kind and number of information codes. At any time that the computer finds that this document is deficient in any logical fashion it will terminate its examination of codes for that document and start anew on codes of the next document. Even if the computer finds that all the question codes are present in the codes for any document the computer still must make further comparison to determine whether or not those information units are additionally topologically or otherwise connectedly related to each other in the manner specified in the question. Some idea of the number and complexity of the necessary intercomparisons may be gained by a realization that documents frequently specify not one but many alternative codes at various points throughout the disclosure, and similarly the questioner may be willing to accept any one of a number of different codes as satisfying any one of the coded units of the question set.

The fourth problem of the computer program is the so-called "check-out routine". Even after the computer has made the necessary comparisons and stored somewhere in its memory a record of which information units and which specified relationships therebetween were found, there is still the problem of evaluating this information and translating it into a form capable of human understanding. This can be a simple printout of the identifying data for each document which fully satisfied the search, or it can be much more complex by causing the computer also suitably to identify those documents which meet certain minimal requirements and give the searcher something not asked for, but which may be pertinent and helpful in case a complete hit is not registered.

While the computer can make these comparisons at electronic speeds, it must be recognized that the programing must be done in such a fashion as to make use of every possible device that will allow the computer immediately to skip over any data which can be determined to be unnecessary to the satisfaction of the search question then being processed. In this way the computer will be more efficiently used and the search time materially reduced.

An Application of an Electronic Computer to Information Retrieval

HARLEY TILLITT

U.S. Naval Ordnance Test Station
China Lake, California

FOR MANY years there has been considerable interest at the U.S. Naval Ordnance Test Station, China Lake, California, in the problems of retrieving information from library files. In addition to the regular services provided by the Technical Library, individuals who worked in areas at some distance from the library or who had special needs associated with particular collections of reports, made use of such systems as Zator, Hadley, and McBee. In addition some "home made" devices were developed and are still in satisfactory operation.

Somewhat before the IBM 701 calculator was installed, the Technical Library had been considering the establishment of the Uniterm System. Considering this level of interest in the retrieval problem including both the library and various individuals, it was natural to expect that some experimentation would be done with the IBM 701 calculator which was delivered in September 1953.

By May 1954 a procedure had been coded for the 701 that mechanized some of the steps which are normally done by hand when using a Uniterm card file. This included a way of inserting information into the system, a means of deleting unwanted information from the system, and the matching of search requests against the master file, with a printout of selected document numbers. After a short period, and independent from any machine requirements, it was clear that certain changes in the system were desirable. These changes included a reworking of the master list of terms to include certain polyterms, a provision for identifying documents with respect to their security classification and point of origin on the Station, as well as their acquisition number. At about the same time it was decided that several improvements should be made in the machine coordination process itself. This improved system was completed early in 1956 and was reported in the April 1957 issue of the *Journal of the Association for Computing Machinery*.

The system has been in use for some time and an evaluation of it is given below. In general, machine searching has not been used very much even though it is estimated by the Station's Technical Library that about 50 per cent of all searching is done by subject with the Uniterm files.

For the most part machine requests include only two or three terms, and for this type of search, the Uniterm files may be quicker and simpler to use than the computer, unless the number of reports per term is too great. Experience with the present machine program and the current file of 25,000 reports, using 12,000 terms with seven to eight terms per report, indicates that unless a request includes five or more terms it will probably not be economical in time to use the computer. (On the other hand, if too many terms are given in a request, there may be no output at all.) Another frequent type of request is that in which only one term is required. This calls for no coordination since it is merely a request for a list of all reports on a given subject.

There are at least two reasons why machine searching has not been put to greater use. One reason, referred to above, has to do with the type of search requests which were made. In some cases the machine cannot show a saving of time. A second reason is more of a psychological one. For example, individuals who want information seem to "want it now", not in three or four hours from now. It seems likely, however, that in many cases the individual knows, hours or maybe even days, ahead, that he is going to search the library for information on his current project. Often, it would have been possible for him to ask his secretary, in advance, to get the information. Also, it is no doubt the case that after many "do it now" searches, the individual does not start immediately to read the reports, but puts them on his desk to look at "the first thing in the morning". Perhaps, however, most of us carry on our own work with this "hurry up and wait" mode of operation. With such an attitude it is natural for an individual to develop a feeling that the machine cannot conduct a search quickly enough. Under other circumstances, what might be called planned searching could be done. That is, all search requests received before noon might be regularly scheduled on the machine for 1.00 P.M. that day, and all search requests made during that afternoon might be completed, on schedule, the following morning at 8.00 A.M. In this way the efficiency of the machine coordination could be demonstrated by making fifty to seventy-five simultaneous searches.

A psychological factor almost opposite to the one mentioned above is that there is a feeling, at first, that the machine can do everything, and when this turns out not to be the case, the system suffers. In other words, after a machine search, when the requestor is given a piece of paper with report numbers printed on it, he seems to forget the great amount of labor he has just been spared if he had had to obtain the same numbers by hand coordination, and laments, "is that all this magic brain can do?"

In 1954 this project was referred to as an Experiment in Information Searching. Since then machine capabilities have been improved by the installation of larger and more reliable memories and better tape systems. Also, some things have been learned about the way people make use of, and respond to, this type of mechanization. The project is still considered to be worth further investigation. Plans are now in progress to reprogram the procedure for the 704 with two objectives in mind: (1) to give greater consideration to the requestor by providing the source, title, date and some idea of the contents of reports, in addition to their acquisition numbers, and (2) to improve the searching speed.

Data Retrieval with Especial Application to Use of Film Library Instantaneous Presentation (FLIP) in Literature Searching

PETER K. WORSLEY

Systems Engineer, Benson–Lehner Co.
Los Angeles, California

EVER SINCE man started using words in order to influence his environment, he has been faced with the twin problems of tracking what has happened and what is going on. The tempo and complexity of life has increased the rate at which decisions are required, resulting in the necessity for indexing information in multidimensional fashion. Concurrently, technological advancements have increased the already copious records, further increasing the searching and selection time.

There is great need for a relatively simple, effective machine which will search film libraries at high speed. Yet, only a few recognized semi-automatic machines have been developed for information retrieval. These machines search by means of cards, magnetic tape, photographic film or combinations of these media. Recognition of descriptors is made through the presence or absence of holes in the cards, magnetized areas on the magnetic tape, and transparent or translucent areas on the photographic film.

These machines have generally increased searching speeds, decreasing search time in the order of one hundredth or more. (Information retrieval is not only concerned with the search for correct information, but also with editing of retrieved information in order to weed out the extraneous documents and obtaining copies where required.)

This brochure describes a photographic film reading machine developed by Benson–Lehner Corporation for this purpose. It has been named FLIP for its prime function: Film Library Instantaneous Presentation.

THE FLIP

The FLIP is an automatic microfilm searching machine designed, built and thoroughly tested. It is a substantial step towards the solution of information retrieval involving large masses of documents. The FLIP was designed for a specific application and not to solve the general information retrieval problem. However, it provides a firm base for further developments; particularly in situations where microfilming techniques would be of great advantage, were it not for the liability of high speed data retrieval where information needs to be searched by descriptors rather than by a simple serial number.

The prime design criterion was to develop a machine to search for a particular frame on 16-mm film at the comparatively high speed of 300 to 600 frames per second—then present this frame for viewing to the operator. Each frame contains pictorial data and binary coded information. The binary coded bits are in the form of black bars on a clear background; thirty-two bits in this case provide all the necessary combinations desired; one group of these bits is used for synchronization pulses. In this particular application the machine is searching for a particular binary number without knowing where it is on the film, except that in one direction numbers are always increasing, although there may be large gaps in the sequence. Upon command to search, the machine chooses the correct direction for search and, upon recognizing the frame, stops, overshoots about five frames and returns to project the image on the screen for visual presentation.

SYSTEM DESCRIPTION

The FLIP is a completely self-contained equipment. No additional components or accessories are required.

The film viewer is designed to locate and display a desired frame in a reel of specially processed 16-mm photographic film. By means of a self-contained keyboard, appropriate indexing information is established. Following this entry, the SEARCH bar is depressed. Release of the SEARCH bar causes the equipment automatically to transport and scan the film until the desired frame has been located. Information contained on the selected frame is projected on the viewing screen. Simultaneously, frame identification, coinciding with the operator entry, is digitally displayed on an illuminated light bank indicator. Thus, frame selection is verified and the operator signalled that a new search may be instituted.

The film transport is designed to accommodate 1200 feet of 16-mm, double perforated film, containing up to 72,000 frames. This footage may be contained on either the supply or takeup reel or distributed in any manner between them. The film itself is scanned at a minimum speed of 60 inches/second. An interval of 1·5 seconds is normally required for the film to attain full scanning speed and decelerate to final stop and display. During the scanning interval, photosensitive elements simultaneously read coded binary digits represented by the presence or absence of code bars adjacent to each film frame presentation. At rest, the desired film frame is positioned before the optical system with an accuracy of ± 10 per cent of the length of the frame (0·2 inch).

The optical system projects a sharp image over the entire field of view with sufficient intensity to permit operation in a normally lighted room. The image is enlarged approximately 50 diameters on the rear of a back-lighted screen without appreciable loss of resolution or contrast. The resolution of the optical system is better than 25 lines/mm.

The direction of the film movement, including initial search direction, is automatically controlled by the film viewer control

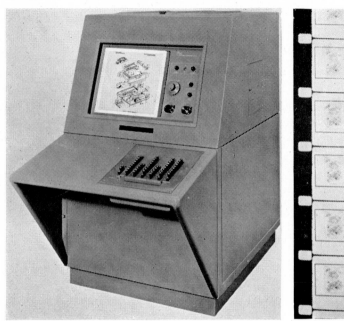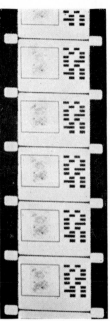

THE FLIP

Film Transport Assembly

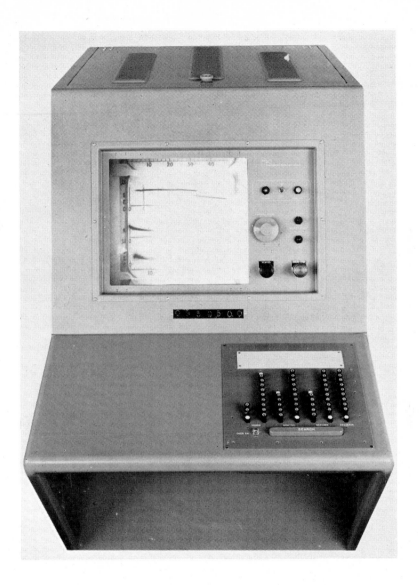

Typical Programed Presentation

Power Supplies and Circuit Boards

units through a comparison of frame and keyboard numbers. When the film is in motion, gated signals produced by reading the moving code bars on the film are supplied to logic modules. These signals are converted and compared with the static keyboard signals. When the desired frame is before the optical gate and all information is stored and converted, a signal is transmitted to the film viewer control units. This actuates a clutch which triggers film reversal and return at a speed of 1·2 inches/second. When the selected frame returns before the optical gate, a supplementary signal stops the film motion.

Circuitry has been incorporated to provide checks and visual indications of such conditions as operating delay, missing frames and faults.

Magnavox Activities in Data Processing

ROBERT HAYES

The Magnavox Company

FOR A number of years the Magnavox Company has been engaged in research, development and manufacturing of data processing equipment. I have been asked by this symposium to describe two of our activities in this area—the Magnacard development and the Minicard development.

THE MINICARD SYSTEM

The following information represents an abstract of data previously presented by Kuipers, Tyler and Myers of the Eastman–Kodak Company in papers in November 1954 and April 1957*. These papers described the development of a Minicard system for the storage and retrieval of information. During the time since then, the development has continued; improved prototype machines have been built; and experience has been gained in operation. The Minicard program is still in a development phase, however, and as yet no decisions have been made with respect to commercial availability of Minicard equipment. At the present, all facilities are committed to prior needs of departments of the government.

* A. W. TYLER, W. L. MYERS and J. W. KUIPERS, The Application of the Kodak Minicard System to Problems of Documentation, *American Documentation*, 6, 18–30 (1955).

J. W. KUIPERS, A. W. TYLER and W. L. MYERS, A Minicard System for Documentary Information, *American Documentation*, 8, 246–268 (1957).

During this development program, the Magnavox Company has made substantial contributions to the design and construction of individual machines, as sub-contractor to Eastman–Kodak. In particular, the design and construction of the Minicard Sorter and of the electronic portion of the Minicard Duplicator were carried out in the Fort Wayne and Los Angeles facilities of Magnavox.

The medium of storage in the Minicard system is the Minicard itself. This card is about 1 in. × $\frac{1}{2}$ in. of acetate, coated with a high resolution photographic emulsion. The development of the emulsion was itself a highly significant factor in the whole Minicard program. In order to meet the general requirements of storage capacity, a virtually unlimited resolution capability was required.

Information is stored on the card either in image form, as an image of a document page, for example, or in coded form, as a coded representation of subject coverage, for example. For these dual purposes, the card has been divided along its length into seven areas, one of which is always dedicated to coded data; the other six can be used either for the storage of coded data or image data. A single one of the six areas has capacity for storage of two document pages, each $8\frac{1}{2}$ × 14, at a 60 to 1 reduction ratio. On the other hand, if devoted to coded data, an area has capacity for 420 bits arranged in ten columns of forty-two bits each. If the entire card, all seven areas, were devoted to coded data, the capacity would be almost 3000 bits. If the maximum area were devoted to image data, the capacity would be 420 bits of coded data and twelve document pages.

The system of Minicard equipment is the set of machines developed to produce the cards and automatically handle them. These machines include the Minicard Camera, Processor, Cutter, Duplicator, Filing Sorter and Selector. The Camera has facility for simultaneously photographing, on a film strip, the coded area and image area for each card. For average documents of six pages with about 200 characters of coded data, the recording rate is forty to fifty documents per hour. The film processor is an automatic photographic developing unit which operates on film strip at about forty Minicards per minute. The Cutter produces individual Minicards from the resulting developed strip at about 600 cards per minute.

The Duplicator has the broad purpose of producing copies of Minicards. However, it has a number of modes of operation, one of which provides the capability of recording on each duplicate card a single column (of forty-two bits) of new data in a fixed area of the card called the Sort Column. This feature is a fundamental part of the entire Minicard system of operation, since it is by use of it that Minicard file copies of a master Minicard are produced. Normally each such file copy will contain in its "sort column" a different column of data from the coded area of the card. The sort column is then used as the control column for sorting into the working Minicard file. The Minicard Duplicator operates at a rate up to 120 Minicards per minute.

The Filing Sorter has the capability of sorting cards on the basis of data located anywhere on the card, although its most important mode of operation uses the sort column. The method of sorting is similar to that of the well-known punched card sorter, in the sense that a single character controls the sort on each pass. The character read from each card then determines into which of ten pockets the card goes. The flexibility of the device has been made appreciably greater than this, however, by providing *two* automatic passes. The first of these operates as described. The second pass allows for selection of one of one hundred pockets rather than just ten. The machines operates at a rate up to 1000 cards per minute (during a single pass).

The Selector uses a transport mechanism very similar to that of the Filing Sorter. However, decision as to which pocket to stack any given card is made on the basis of the entire coded area of the card rather than just a single character. The Selector has associated with it a sophisticated logical unit which processes the entire set of data read from the card in order to arrive at a decision on what to do with the card. The Selector operates at a rate up to 1200 cards per minute.

The system of operation for which Minicard has been designed is based on the storage of multiple copies of a given document— one copy for each subject coverage of the document on which recovery at some later time may be desired. In addition to this, it was required that the logical processes for recovery should be very sophisticated, allowing for grouping of the data in the coded area into phrases, each of which could be treated as an independent logical unit.

In summary, the system of operation involves the storage in the coded area of each card of a multiplicity of codes for use in later recovery of the document. Multiple copies—one for each code on which specific recovery may later be desired—are prepared on the Duplicator, each one with the corresponding code added in the Sort Column. The resulting file copies are then sorted into the master file on the basis of the sort column.

For recovery of documents according to some set of criteria, one code from the set is used to select a group of cards from the file —those cards with that code in the sort column. The group of cards is then scanned by the selector, and the coded data from each card compared with the whole set of criteria. In making this comparison, the logic can be extremely complicated and sophisticated. Conditions of logical "and", "or", and "not" can be applied to the data from the card. In doing so, the data from the card can be considered as a unit or as a group of independent phrases.

THE MAGNACARD SYSTEM

The following information represents an abstract of data previously presented in various papers during 1957*. The Magnacard development was undertaken to develop equipment to solve in an efficient and economic manner routine data handling problems, including the operations of sorting, selecting, merging, file searching and input–output. A second objective was to develop extremely high-capacity memory systems with eraseable storage and with rapid access either in a sequential or in a random manner. The approach chosen to meet these objectives centered around the use of discrete magnetic cards where the cards themselves, rather than

---

* J. WIENER, "Magnacard—A New High-Speed Filing System", ACM Meeting, June 1957, Houston, Texas.

R. THORENSEN, "The Magnacard Development", AIEE Meeting, June 1957, Montreal, Quebec.

R. M. HAYES and J. WIENER, "Magnacard—A New Concept in Data Handling", WESCON Convention, August 1957, San Fransico, California.

A. M. NELSON, H. M. STERN and L. R. WILSON, "Magnacard—Mechanical Handling Techniques", WESCON Convention, August 1957, San Francisco, California.

the information recorded on the cards, were sorted, merged, etc. This approach required the development of equipment capable of handling magnetic cards efficiently and rapidly.

The unit record chosen consists of a magnetic card measuring 1 in. × 3 in., having a storage capacity of more than 5000 binary digits. The card is of sandwich-type construction, consisting of a 5-mil thick Mylar base, approximately ½-mil thick layer of magnetic oxide and binder mixture, and a ½-mil thick Mylar overlay. The three layers are bonded together by a laminating process to yield a card with extremely rugged mechanical characteristics. This card will withstand heavy usage under operating conditions without damage or appreciable wear. Information is recorded on the card in eighteen parallel channels at a linear density of 100 binary digits per inch. The techniques used for reading and recording data on these cards are similar to those presently used with magnetic drums.

The card handling transport equipment involves the use of vacuum transport drums, card feeding-stacking stations, and card transfer devices. The heart of the transport system is the vacuum drum. This drum is 8 in. in diameter, 1 in. wide and rotates at a constant speed of twelve revolutions per second. The interior of the drum is hollow and connects through a hollow shaft to a vacuum pump. The periphery of the drum is slotted to connect with the hollow interior so that vacuum can be applied continuously to the drum periphery through these slots. When a card is placed on the periphery of the drum, it is held firmly in place by the pressure differential existing between the interior and the exterior of the drum. In effect, the card now behaves like the magnetic surface of any magnetic drum memory system. To make this device useful, means have been provided for feeding magnetic cards on to the drum surface and for stacking cards from the drum. This is accomplished with reversible feed-stack stations; either of these functions can be selected automatically. The cards are fed on to the drum automatically, either singly or continuously. In the stations, the cards are held in special removable Magnacard trays, each of 3000 cards maximum capacity.

The operations of sorting, merging, etc., demand that a single card may be routed along any one of a number of possible card paths so that the cards may be separated into groups. This is accomplished through the use of two or more vacuum transport drums placed adjacent to each other with the added capability of being able to transfer a card from one drum to the next. These transfer devices operate by applying an air jet tangentially to the drum to literally blow the edge of the card from the surface of one drum to the surface of an adjacent drum. The air jet is controlled by a fast acting electrodynamic valve to achieve individual and selective card transfer.

All the above operations of transporting, feeding, stacking and selective card transfer take place at card rates up to 100 cards per second with the cards being transported on the drums at speeds of 300 inches per second. This very high transport speed, combined with the flexibility of being able to control the path that the card takes to achieve sorting and merging, constitutes perhaps the strongest advantage of the system. The high transport speed also yields high rates of reading and writing of information on to the magnetic storage medium. Information rates of 100,000 decimal digits per second can be achieved easily.

Techniques have also been worked out for the mechanization of very high capacity files. One technique involves arranging Magnacard trays, each of three million decimal digit storage capacity, into a vertical array of ten trays, with a resulting total capacity of over 30 million decimal digits. The array may be automatically positioned to insert any tray into a feed-stack station of a drum transport assembly.

For applications requiring larger files of cards automatically available, a file mechanism is being developed which arranges Magnacard trays into a rectangular block of seven by fifteen trays, giving a total capacity of over 300 million decimal digits. The block may be automatically positioned to insert any tray into a feed-stack station of a drum transport assembly. To gain access to a specific card within a tray, the drum transport assembly passes the cards at the rate of 100 per second past a reading station until the proper item is found. The time for positioning the block, tray insertion and extraction and card transport takes on the average of 30 seconds.

When a shorter random access time is desirable, a second technique has been worked out involving the sidewise extraction from a tray of a small group of cards and the insertion of these cards into a drum transport assembly for reading. The number of cards scanned at a time is approximately 100. By again arranging the card trays into a block structure accessible to a drum transport assembly through a side extraction-insertion mechanism, access to any of 120 million decimal digits may be had in less than 5 seconds.

SYSTEM CONSIDERATIONS

I have described these two developments in general terms, rather than in terms of their application to specific problems. The information presented has therefore been technical data about the characteristics of the storage media and the handling equipments, rather than detailed descriptions of systems of operation.

I wish to emphasize that in doing so, it was not intended to underestimate the importance of systems of operation. This is an area of fundamental concern, and it should be of overlapping interest between the technician and the user. The most efficient system of operation requires an appropriate mating between the characteristics of equipment and the requirements of the job.

Arriving at an optimum system above all requires good communication between the technician and the user. One aspect of this communication was the purpose of my talk today—the description by the technician of the characteristics of equipment. Another aspect is the description, by the potential user of equipment, of his needs. Once this communication—of capabilities on the one hand and of needs on the other—has been established, the mutual development of systems of operation can be initiated.

Because of the importance of common understanding in this area of system of operation, I would like to outline some of the relevant considerations which I feel are important.

The first consideration is the need to distinguish very carefully between those potential benefits in a system which result from the storage medium and its handling equipment as opposed to those which result from the system of operation. In this respect, for example, it has become a truism in the data processing business that an improved *system* of operation, installed as preparation for a computer, frequently results in savings all by itself. On the other hand, it is equally true that the speed and capability of a computing device can be used to mask deficiencies in the system of operation.

The second consideration is the need to distinguish very carefully between the effects of the various elements of a system of operation. The relative costs and benefits of (1) the file organization, (2) the techniques for entry of information, (3) the handling of information during entry, organization, searching, etc., (4) the degree of logical complexity provided, and (5) the methods for output and display —these must be weighed, evaluated and compared with each other. The benefits and difficulties arising from each of these elements must be clearly distinguished and understood.

Finally, the third consideration is the need to distinguish very carefully between the problems as seen by the technician and the problems as seen by the user. That these two viewpoints are frequently confused is evidenced by the typical controversies occurring between the proponents of various specialized approaches. The difficulty arises from the fact that the two aspects—the technician's and the user's—seem to have areas of overlap. In actuality, however, the objectives and methods of each group are vastly different. The apparent similarity of interest leads only to controversy and mutual confusion. This third consideration is a fundamental one, because the area of *legitimate* overlap of interest between the technician and the user—the communication and quantification of user requirements—must be elevated to its true level of importance.

PANEL
DISCUSSION

Planning
for the Future

Opening Statement

by MERRITT L. KASTENS

Assistant Director
Stanford Research Institute

I HAVE been introduced very gracefully as the representative of management on this panel. I think that is appropriate. My interest in the technical information problem can be stated very simply, if somewhat crudely. It costs too much for what we are getting. And let me explain that a little more—because the statement has been made repeatedly in the last few days that these big machines which Dr. Grosch talks about are too expensive. They are *not* too expensive. A poor system that does not do the job it is intended to do *is* too expensive, no matter how little it costs—and our present system is not doing the job it is intended to do. A good system that produces a valid and economic product is cheap no matter how much it costs.

Let me make another point that I don't think has been dealt with in these sessions, a point which I think all of us are inclined to forget in dealing with the particulars of the mechanisms we are discussing. It is simply this: Have you stopped to consider what you *might* do with a really effective technical information system? What are the creative possibilities that are available to us with some of the systems and some of the mechanisms that we can envisage at this point? It isn't sufficient in our thinking to simply solve the present problem. It isn't sufficient merely to find a better or a cheaper way to do what we are doing now. There are a great many things that are not being done which might be done, and which a really good, well thought out, well integrated technical information system could achieve. And remember, when I say a good system, I mean by definition a cheap system; cheap in terms of the value it produces, cheap in terms of the product it presents to its users. Think for a minute of a capability that would allow any member of the faculty on this campus to take some wild idea—some obscure esoteric notion of a correlation between certain concepts—and enable him quickly, and within a reasonable economic cost, to search not the literature of physics, or psychology, or any one field, but to search the entire organized knowledge of the world in all fields to see if this particular conceptual pattern has somehow been reproduced by some other thoughtful man somewhere in the world at some time. This is actually a pretty naive example, but it is the kind of thing of which I am thinking. I think we have an opportunity here, if we will break ourselves out of some conceptual ruts, not only to meet an immediate and apparent problem, but to provide a new creative tool; a new capability for productive intellectual effort of the entire world. I think we have to keep this in mind. It makes the problem more fun if for no other reason. But it is a real, attainable objective. I commend it to your consideration.

Panel Discussion

by Mrs. JOHANNA E. TALLMAN

Engineering Library
University of California, Los Angeles

I SHALL try to summarize how university libraries might fit into the documentation picture.

Many university librarians are afraid of mechanical contrivances and question whether a "true" librarian should even think about information retrieval or documentation. They would be surprised at some of the comments which have been made here and in the academic personnel involved in information and its retrieval. Besides mathematicians and engineers, whom we would expect to be involved, there are, for example, linguists, grammarians, philosophers, psychologists, physicists, and logicians.

It seems to me that university librarians should be aware of the interests of these people and should be prepared to help answer their questions by having pertinent books, documents, and periodicals in the university library. Librarians should also know something about inexpensive, relatively uncomplicated methods of information retrieval such as edge-notched cards or coordinate index systems. These can be used in the library for circulation systems, serial records, and indexes to pamphlets and special collections. Librarians can also help the faculty, students, or research people to set up such systems for their own collections and files.

Several speakers have emphasized that machines are only part of the information retrieval picture and that programing for machines still requires intellectual effort such as judgment, intuition, and creative thinking. A university is usually thought of as a center of intellectual activity, and the library is always spoken of as the heart of the university. It seems, therefore, that university librarians should not ignore information retrieval as a phase of intellectual activity.

Universities might follow the example of Western Reserve University, which has indexed metal literature, by indexing mathematics, electronics, physics, and other subject literature that exist in vast quantities and are in great demand. If each cooperating university would make its index available, on exchange or sale, many people would have access to all of this indexed information.

In addition, complete literature texts put on film, minicards, microcards, FLIP, or other forms are *always* available; they are never "at the bindery" or "out in circulation".

Documentation machines are expensive, but this problem can be solved if several industries and/or universities in an area cooperate in the use or expense of a machine.

To summarize, then, a university library definitely fits into the documentation picture. Inasmuch as the various procedures of documentation require intellectual effort, it is logical that the university library, the heart of a community's intellectual center, should cooperate in experiments with progressive methods of retrieving information quickly.

Panel Discussion

by EDWIN CASTAGNA

City Librarian,
Long Beach Public Library

PLANNING FOR THE FUTURE
IN PUBLIC LIBRARIES

I AM interested in Mr. Grosch's idea for culturing organisms to do the retrieval job. But I am a little disappointed that he stopped short at the point where they would say, "Here I am". Why can't they line up in the order of their ability to solve the problem? And then why not have them infiltrate the brain cells of the documentalist by a kind of osmosis? This would be real programing. Let's not stop at half measures!

Not many documentalists, or special librarians, can be expected to read the little magazine called the *Wilson Library Bulletin*, so they wouldn't know of Harry Bauer's article on documentation in the March 1958 issue. He begins, "Documentation is in great vogue among those gentle souls who wish to add to the confusion of knowledge; and documentalists have endeavored, with indifferent success, to change their vocation into a profession by inventing a jargon replete with such absurd phrases as retrieval of information, trope indexing, uniterm, correlative indexing, non-manipulative index, and coordinate indexing." Mr. Bauer then goes on to point out some of the pitfalls of documentation. His tone is acid sometimes but he seems to be writing partly in fun—your rather skeptical, rueful sounding laughter reminds me of the man who was telling a lady that women always seemed to take everything so personally. She answered rather sharply, "Well, *I* don't!" Anyway, public librarians

G 89

as well as university librarians like Mr. Bauer may be expected to react cautiously to the promises of the computer and its fellow devices.

This may be partly due to the fact that in considering possible applications of the techniques of documentation in public libraries, we know that public librarians are, on the whole, generalists, while documentation is highly specialized. What kind of mechanical device could be built to answer in turn and very rapidly (as we must every day do in a public library) questions like these: How many air miles is it from Reno to San Francisco? What is the market for Thermos bottles in Afghanistan? What is the per capita income in Long Beach? How can I take my cat's temperature? Who was president of Venezuela in 1947? Was Little Jack Horner a real person? What is the name of the leading woman character in "Cat on a Hot Tin Roof" and what was her problem? Those of you who are public librarians know this is the way questions come. Now what machine will answer these questions that come helter-skelter, diverse and unanticipated, to which the answers are wanted immediately? An important business decision may depend on a prompt and accurate answer. Or maybe there are a couple of fellows drinking in a bar and have a bet on. Or a writer is up against a deadline and needs a fact in a hurry. These people can't wait until the machine is programed. The public librarian himself is the information retrieval device. He is programed over a period of many years, through his whole education, during his experience on the job and away from it. No idea fed into him in completely lost.

And he doesn't need to be rewired for every new problem.

Therefore, I think that it would be well at this stage for public librarians to watch carefully and try to understand as much as they can about developments in documentation. Someone in every public library should be keeping track of what is going on. Then he can feed that knowledge into his organization and suggest possible applications. This I think is a minimum responsibility for public libraries.

Most of you know that public libraries are increasingly becoming mechanized. We use photographic equipment, microfilm, punched cards, and many other labor-saving and work-simplifying devices. And we will probably continue to investigate and acquire more of them. However, because of the great costs and the extremely technical problems that only very expert specialists can solve, I believe public libraries should look, as Mrs. Tallman has suggested, in the direction of cooperation. It does seem important to me that public libraries, which serve the broadest segment of our population, should be ready to put their facilities cooperatively to use in bringing technical and scientific information to all those who may find it useful. There seems to be a danger of a kind of monopoly in this field under which individuals and small interests will be excluded from highly profitable information that should really be in the public domain because it is often developed at public cost. Perhaps centers could be organized, in which documentalists might be gathered with their machines and equipment, to which individual libraries might belong, either as subscribers or by paying for a service as it is provided. Or possibly the government, on some level, might create a system of regional centers or one center as part of the national library system.

These are some of the documentation responsibilities and possibilities in the future of public libraries. We should keep fully informed of developments. We should use that which appears to be useful in performing our important information function. And we should be ready as a nationwide system of public agencies to keep technical communication channels open to all and not limited to a privileged few.

Panel Discussion

by JOHN SINCLAIR

Hughes Aircraft Company

IT would be interesting to look for a moment at the potential market for information retrieval systems and to discover where financial support may originate for research in this field.

Today we have heard discussion of the public library and the small industrial technical library where the consumers of information are, respectively, the public and the technical industrial staff. Of these two groups, the industrial technical library is backed by the strongest economic motive and capability to improve its services. The universities have many fine libraries, both general and technical, but only few can afford to do more than sniff in the direction of automation. In the legal profession, a difficult and expensive part of litigation is in the preparation of briefs of the past decisions which bear on the case at hand. The legal profession may well be interested in support for research in the automation of the law libraries, since attorneys are aware of the great expense and delay which present-day legal procedures can entail. Here again is an economic motivation.

The medical profession could use a good diagnostic machine into which the doctor feeds the symptoms and out of which come the names and cures, if any, for the most probable diseases which could have produced the symptoms observed. Here the impetus to improve their services may lead various medical organizations to sponsor research into the design of such diagnostic machines. I understand that Johns Hopkins medical school has done some work in this direction.

The business world has already discovered what the use of machine-business-methods can do for them and are even now developing various new mechanized information-gathering agencies to assist them. One can imagine a ready market for information searching systems which, for example, give transportation data or source-of-supply data "on demand". Research and development in this field is sponsored primarily by the business machines industry which, of course, will become the supplier of these retrieval machines.

Much interest in automatic information retrieval is being generated at present within that part of industry which does military research and development. These industries realize the tremendous waste involved in re-doing research which has already been done. In order to assist their contractors, the military services employ an organization called ASTIA (Armed Services Technical Information Agency) for collecting, searching, and distributing all contractual reports on work done by or for the military. This agency is in dire need of modernization of its services. The complete change in methods called for would be quite expensive and might be difficult to justify to Congress or some other source of government support. However, the importance of automatic retrieval would be so great that we may soon see increased pressure in this direction. Development of an automatic retrieval system for ASTIA would have useful side effects if the results of this development become available generally. It is hoped that research on information retrieval systems done for the armed services will be published so that non-military organizations throughout the U.S. may benefit.

It is clear then that economics will play a dominant role in the development of machine retrieval systems. We can expect rapid progress in those areas in which the money for research is available. We hope that the results of this research will become generally available to U.S. industry as rapidly as possible and that such independent research organizations as RAND, Western Reserve, and Stanford Research Institute will continue to contribute not only specific technical work, but a measure of broad guidance in the present deep forest of information retrieval systems.

Panel Discussion

by Dr. JOHN GERLETTI

Associate Professor, School of Public Administration
University of Southern California

THE problem that we are dealing with today is probably the most important problem facing the education world at the present time. This problem is, how to sift out that information which is good and to make it available when it is needed.

With the ever increasing amount of information which is being turned out today, and the speed with which the world is changing, knowledge becomes more and more valuable and also more difficult to get.

We in Public Administration, a new discipline, are interested in not just the knowledge of the field of management but we are also interested in the knowledge of all of the related fields and especially those fields of the behavioral sciences.

Much comment has been made of late to the effect that the physical sciences are taking a tremendous lead in the research efforts of the world and that behavioral sciences and other fields of endeavor are losing out. This may be true to a point, but it is also important to recognize the fact that many of the other fields can utilize the techniques, knowledges, and skills which are developed in the research approaches of the physical sciences. Especially would this be true in terms of utilization of electronic data processing equipment in the storage and recall of knowledge.

However, I would definitely like to raise some questions today:

1. What yardstick of efficiency did the United States use before the Russians put the first Sputnik into orbit?

2. For what purpose, long range purpose that is, are we so interested in the process of collecting material and putting it on memory drums and storing it so it can be recalled?

3. Is it possible to develop a common language in this field rather than the unique language which all of you have been using here at this meeting? If the results of your efforts are to be picked up by the other disciplines and by other users it must be made in language that can be understood by other people.

4. What impact upon college education will the use of these modern devices for the storage and recall of information have? How will we have to redesign our total educational program; first, to make use of these techniques and second, to extend our knowledge beyond that which we already have?

5. I would like to challenge a statement which has been made today; that only the man with money will have information available to him. This is a dangerous thought. If you recall, the American Postal System was based upon the original concept that information should be made available to all people, therefore, the second, third, and fourth class rates.

6. It appears there is an ethical problem involved in the availability of information and the utilization of this information. As a person who is in the public service, I am interested in the problem of public interest. Would it be possible to have government subsidies in the storage of knowledge? We do this with the Library of Congress. This could be another extension of the Library of Congress service.

7. It is possible to raise another question at this point. To what extent is this coding and decoding of information blocking the progress of additional information?

I would like to see a committee from this organization or a committee of librarians systematically work out a series of basic questions that should be asked in relationship to this problem. This would make it possible to have the benefit of some of the great minds in the country on this most important problem.

Panel Discussion

by Dr. WILLIS H. WARE

The RAND Corporation
Santa Monica, California

As near as I can tell, there are three kinds of people represented in the audience this afternoon. There is a set of people who have been in the data processing business for a long time in one way or another; there are a few people whose interest in data retrieval seems to be tangential, or of the nature of a hobby; and the balance of the people here are those who wish somebody would do something about their problem—these are the librarians who have to retrieve data. I would like to direct my comments just to the librarians.

Nobody would deny that the library problem is a difficult one. There are two ways that one can get at the solution. The first would be to theorize about the problem until the solution is known so perfectly that the perfect device to deal with it can be described. The risk here is that the remaining years that this earth has to live might not be enough to see it through.

The other possibility is that one experiments in any profitable direction that can be seen. For the librarian, this could be risky also, because what could happen is that everyone would have a system unto himself and these systems might not communicate conveniently. So the interlibrary problem might then become very nasty.

There is clearly indicated some balance between experimentation and theorizing. A pertinent question seems to me to be "Whose obligation is it to worry about implementation of active work?" I'm not overly familiar with the professional organizations that serve the library industry, but there must be one that plays "mother" to it.

It seems to me that this professional organization has some obligations which it ought to face up to if it hasn't already. One of these is standardization. Other industries have said to themselves, "Mechanization is on the way, and we had better start now to get ready for it". The American Banking Association, for instance, has already decided that certain things must be true of any equipment which is to be used within its industry, and I suspect that it is about time for the library organization to begin to compose some sort of preliminary statements about what it would be willing to accept from vendors of equipment.

To a large extent the equipment designers have leap-frogged in front of most of the applications. In seeking new markets the equipment suppliers look at problems in various fields, but not being experts of long standing in a potential field of application, not all of the really involved or subtle aspects of the application are likely to be understood by them. There is no need really why such vendors should be wholly educated into the problems of an industry which has a problem. It seems to me that basically this is the responsibility of that industry. It should at least know what problems it wants solved.

It seems to me also that the professional organization of the industry ought to have an obligation to encourage experimentation, and cross-fertilization of the several people who are experimenting. It seems to me that the professional organization has an obligation to look into itself and try to understand what basic processes are concerned with the industry it represents—to understand what really goes on in a library, not what superficially goes on. Then it must state these problems in a fashion which makes sense to those people who can provide mechanized equipment to deal with them.

There is a platitude that is often passed around at a meeting that deals with data processing, but hasn't yet appeared at this one, so I think it's worth my contributing it. The statement is made at many meetings concerned with data processing problems: "What you fellows really have is a man-machine problem!" This is particularly true in the library. In directing your thoughts to solutions which might be acceptable, I think it very clear that the interaction between the machine and the man must not be overlooked. If it is, then I think the resulting solution would prove unacceptable.

97

I'd like also to observe that meetings of the nature of this one are an extremely healthy sign. Invariably a potential user of data processing equipment does not fully understand his problem at the outset. Only when he begins to discuss it with a supplier of equipment does he truly begin to understand and formulate the problem in a workable and realistic fashion. I'm sure that much of this is occurring during this symposium.

Panel Discussion

by EUGENE M. GRABBE

Senior Staff Consultant on Automation
The Ramo-Wooldridge Corporation

In PLANNING for the future of information retrieval systems, there are three points I would like to discuss briefly. Since my background is in the technical field, these comments are oriented toward automatic equipment and are concerned with (a) automatic abstracting and indexing, (b) feedback processes, and (c) new developments for storage and computing.

Automatic abstracting has been accomplished on an experimental basis as reported to you by Mr. Luhn of IBM. It would also be desirable to have indexing done automatically. When technical people prepare indexes they do not do an adequate job because they do not have the time, the interest, or the knowledge of how to index properly. Librarians, on the other hand, do not have the technical knowledge for indexing scientific literature. Hence, machine indexing and abstracting would be desirable. An intermediate step would be to obtain more participation from engineers and scientists in abstracting and indexing.

Use of feedback in information retrieval systems may be of very great importance. Feedback consists of taking information concerning the output of a system and using this to improve the operation of the system. First of all, feedback is necessary to improve any documentation system. The user must advise the system operators as to whether he is receiving the information required in a reasonable time. This evaluation of the system (feedback) can then be used to improve the operation. This concept becomes very important when automatic equipment is used for information retrieval.

The forms of feedback might take in automatic documentation as follows: (1) A user might request the system to provide a sample of the documents he has requested. He can then look these over and decide whether he has made the proper request. If not, a new request is fed back to the machine to provide the required information output. (2) A user might also want to know how many items an automatic system will produce for a given request. An automatic system could then scan the files and come up with a statistical indication predicting how many items would be supplied for the request. If this number is too large or too small, feedback from the requestor can again modify the request and narrow down or broaden the range of subject material.

The present high cost of automatic storing and filing systems has been mentioned. To give an example of present cost, if we were today to put all the information in the Library of Congress (estimated at 10^{14} bits) on magnetic tapes, the cost of the tapes alone would be 100 million dollars. If equipment was employed so that all these tapes were attached to a computer for use, the total cost of tapes and equipment would be 100 billion dollars. Another form of storage is magnetic cores and for this type of storage system, the cost would be 100 trillion dollars. Hence, at present we can consider only the storing of indexes in machines as economically feasible. With advances in technology, there will be a time in the future when, with automatic abstracting, indexing, and information retrieval, we can anticipate that all the information in books and journals will be put into a storage system.

These storage cost figures lead to a final point concerning the need for improvements in equipment and devices for automatic documentation. Large capacity, fast, random-access, and cheap storage devices will be required. New technical developments are needed since the present techniques and devices are too expensive. Perhaps some new form of computer is also required for information retrieval and documentation systems. So far, the work has been done mainly on general purpose machines, designed for mathematical computations. It is possible that a specific urgent problem, such as that of the requirements of documentation, may produce some new approach. A computer for documentation should be something that works very much like the human system: a combination of parallel and serial operations with a considerable amount of redundancy.

The future growth of automatic documentation systems on a broad scale will depend upon the technical developments since present techniques are too expensive. Intermediate steps may lie in the partial application of automation and in new approaches that result from cross-fertilization between the representatives of the libraries and technical fields.

Index

This symposium was sponsored by the School of Library Science of the University of Southern California to stimulate interest in information retrieval. Due to the increase in knowledge and the vast quantity of published material, the matter of keeping fully informed, however specialized the field, has become an enormous problem to specialists, research workers and librarians. Questions of documentation and information retrieval are constantly being posed and much individual research is in progress. To meet this need a new technology is being evolved employing mechanised systems for searching, correlating and synthesising data. The participants, of diverse background and widely varying institutions, discussed the individual needs of libraries served by information retrieval systems, problems of locating information, mechanical translation by automatic computers and language data processing, automatic encoding and data retrieval by microfilm, magnacard and minicard.

The volume will stimulate interest and accelerate progress in this increasingly important field and will prove essential reading to all concerned with university, industrial and research laboratory libraries.